A Practical Guide to Enrollment and Retention Management in Higher Education

Marguerite J. Dennis

D0002389

BERGIN & GARVEY
Westport, Connecticut • London

Library of Congress Cataloging-in-Publication Data

Dennis, Marguerite J., 1946–
    A practical guide to enrollment and retention management in higher
    education / Marguerite J. Dennis.
        p.   cm.
    Includes bibliographical references (p.) and index.
    ISBN 0–89789–591–6 (alk. paper)
    1. College attendance—United States.   2. College dropouts—United
States—Prevention.   3. College students—Recruiting—United States.
4. Public relations—Universities and colleges—United States.
I. Title.
LC148.2.D45   1998
378.1′694—DC21   98–9532

British Library Cataloguing in Publication Data is available.

Library of Congress Catalog Card Number: 98–9532
ISBN: 0–89789–591–6

First published in 1998

Bergin & Garvey, 88 Post Road West, Westport, CT 06881
An imprint of Greenwood Publishing Group, Inc.

Printed in the United States of America

The paper used in this book complies with the
Permanent Paper Standard issued by the National
Information Standards Organization (Z39.48–1984).

10 9 8 7 6 5 4 3 2 1

Copyright Acknowledgments

The author and publisher gratefully acknowledge permission for the use of the following material:

Robert Topor, *Marketing Higher Education—A Practical Guide.* Washington, D.C.: Council for Advancement and Support of Education, 1983. Quotations reprinted with permission from the author.

Marketing Publication Planning Form created by Robert Topor of Topor Consultants Group International is reprinted with permission from Robert Topor.

Dedicated to
David J. Sargent,
President, Suffolk University
for giving me the freedom to fail and the encouragement to succeed.

Contents

Preface

"Our colleges are not filled because we do not furnish the education desired by the people. We have produced an article for which demand is diminishing. We sell it at less than cost, and the deficiency is made up by charity. We give it away, and the demand still diminishes."

—Francis Wayland, President, Brown University, 1850

In the September, 1989 issue of *Change* magazine, Richard Chait, Executive Director of the National Center for Postsecondary Governance and Finance at the University of Maryland, describes the following memorandum:

To: The Dean of Enrollment Management
From: President (or Faculty Senate)

Welcome aboard. Please recruit more and better students from a smaller and weaker pool of prospects without increased costs, more financial aid, or drastic program changes. Would like to see results reflected in next year's class. Best wishes.

While some administrators may smile at the veiled sarcasm of this statement, there are many enrollment managers who, at some point in their careers, have been given a similar directive or have been told it is their responsibility to fix a school's enrollment problems *now*. Weekly, the *Chronicle of Higher Education* lists newly created or recently vacated positions for enrollment managers. Con-

ferences and seminars sponsor "breakthroughs" in student enrollment. Consultants, offering assurances of increased enrollment to presidents and deans, travel
the country. Research articles present scenarios for guaranteed enrollment success.

The simple fact is that there are more spaces in some of our colleges and universities than there are qualified students. Only 17% of all college students
enroll in private colleges and universities. Many private schools are chasing
after the same students and have been for the past fifteen years.

The truth is that no one knows, with absolute certainty, what makes a student enroll at a particular college or university or why that same student may
decide to leave the school. If a simple formula existed, we would all follow it
so that at our colleges and universities' enrollment problems would diminish,
and attrition rates would decrease. But no such formula exists and probably
never will.

There can be as many effective enrollment and retention management programs as there are institutions of higher education. While each is different and
specific to the student population and campus culture it serves, there are some
basic elements in all successful programs which can be studied, modified,
adapted, implemented, or copied. That is what this book will attempt to do: to
suggest practical and universal ways to approach the enrollment and retention of
students. Although based on research, the suggestions presented in this publication approach enrollment and retention management from a *basic* and *practical*
point of view. These are not my views alone. The recommendations outlined
in this book represent over thirty years of higher education administration experience at St. John's University in New York, a large, suburban university;
Georgetown University School of Dentistry, in Washington, D.C., a professional school; and Suffolk University in Boston, a small, private, urban institution. These opinions are also the result of conducting and participating in many
workshops and seminars. Without exception, my colleagues at other schools
told me that this is the kind of information they need and want.

It is my intention to have this book serve as a tool for practicing enrollment
managers, retention managers, admission directors, financial aid administrators,
registrars, and institutional researchers. This book could also serve as a resource
for non-practitioners, including college and university presidents, provosts,
treasurers, and faculty. It is my belief that enrollment and retention management can only be effective when the entire campus community is engaged and
encouraged to practice its principles and practices.

As a higher education administrator I have been responsible for undergraduate
and graduate admission, financial aid, registration and retention. I feel qualified
to share my successes and failures with you because I have experienced both. I
have made every mistake there is to make. However, I have tried not to make
the same mistake twice. I am not a professional consultant, marketing guru,
computer whiz, or research specialist. I am a *practicing* and *practical* enrollment and retention manager with programs which are works-in-progress. I hope
this will always be the case. Like most people, I am struggling with my con-

stant companion, *change*, and how to incorporate change in a non-threatening way to the campus culture I serve. I constantly feel the need to serve two masters: the university's historic mission and the needs and wants of the students of the next century. My turf battles and customer service issues are probably similar to yours. Like you, I am eager to learn, to grow, and to share my knowledge. I trust that after reading this book you will agree with me that I have been successful in doing that.

Acknowledgments

My sincere appreciation to my former colleagues and friends at St. John's University in New York and Georgetown University School of Dentistry in Washington, D.C. Special thanks to the outstanding enrollment and retention managment team at Suffolk University in Boston for helping me to learn and forcing me to "step out of the box."

A Practical Guide to Enrollment and Retention Management in Higher Education

Introduction

"We are witnessing today the twilight of the four year liberal arts program."

—Journal of Higher Education, 1938

In a 1994 survey of college administrators conducted by the American Council on Education, 62% indicated that enrollment challenges will be one of the most important factors facing their schools in the next four years. We can guess the reasons—a changing United States economy and society, changing demographics, changing technology, changes in federal and state financial aid policies—in a word, change.

The college and university of tomorrow will be very different from the school of today. The number of "traditional" college students, aged sixteen to twenty-four, will probably not be the majority of students in our classrooms. Tomorrow's college students are likely to be older, female, minority and studying part-time. Many will consider English their second language. Some will want to be taught at their work sites, or in their homes. Others will come to the campus in the evening and on the weekend. Many will enroll in courses for most of their working lives. They will demand programs offered at convenient times and at a reasonable price. All will want to be treated as valued customers. They will flock to those schools that meet their needs and abandon the ones that do not. All this means *change*. The faces sitting in college classrooms will change, and this means that the way higher education is delivered in the future will be different from the way it is delivered today.

Enter the enrollment and retention managers, charged with the responsibility of two functions: enrolling qualified students and successfully retaining and graduating them. These are the administrators who are expected to solve all of the enrollment problems at their schools. These are the administrators who are blamed or fired if enrollment targets are not met. These are the managers most often at odds with the faculty, the athletic department, alumni groups, and prospective students and their families. Enrollment and retention management is one of the most difficult and least understood functions on college campuses today. Enrollment and retention managers often find themselves in situations where no constituency is pleased and the "quick fix" is simply not possible. However, I believe that for a majority of colleges and universities these two, intertwined functions are more than tangentially needed to ensure a school's enrollment successes.

Thirty years ago, when I began my career in higher education administration, we didn't call the work we did in admissions, financial aid and registration "enrollment management." But it was. The process has become much more sophisticated than it was at St. John's University in New York in 1966. However, the objectives remain today what they were then: to enroll the most suitable students—students who fulfilled the stated mission and objectives—and to help these students succeed in reaching their educational and career goals.

Enrollment management is a "big business" today. The same can be said for retention management. There are several corporations founded to serve as advisors to the higher education community. Many colleges and universities utilize the services of expensive consultants, fearful of the consequences if they do not. There is some justification for this. Since 1980, over 900 colleges and universities have closed their doors or merged with other institutions. In some cases these schools were no longer able to offer their students the courses or programs demanded by the marketplace. Not even the best enrollment and retention management program can save a school that cannot or will not meet the needs of its student-customers.

Efficient and responsive enrollment and retention management programs can help to solve a school's enrollment problems. However, these two programs cannot act in isolation. A school's president and other senior staff members, the faculty, the institutional advancement people, the accountants and financial personnel, all must work with the enrollment and retention manager to make the programs succeed. Hard choices, usually driven by a lack of resources, have to be made.

Basic Premises Regarding Enrollment and Retention Management

1. There can be no successful enrollment management program without a successful retention management program.
2. There can be no successful enrollment management program without faculty involvement.

3. An enrollment management program can market only what the school has to offer. Perception must match reality.

4. A school's financial aid program will significantly affect its enrollment and retention management program.

5. Enrollment management and retention management should stress goals and focus on accountability and measured outcomes.

6. No one has established with absolute certainty why students select to enroll, or decide to leave, a school. There are economic, geographic, sociological, psychological, and intellectual reasons associated with enrollment and retention. There can be no one perfect program.

7. It should take at least three years to implement a successfull enrollment and retention management program. Fine tuning and refining the programs should be a never-ending and on-going process.

8. To be successful, a school's enrollment and retention management program must match a school's culture and "personality."

9. A school's enrollment and retention management staff is not solely responsible for the program's success or failure. Enrollment and retention management is the responsibility of all campus administrators, staff, and faculty.

10. There is not a lot of magic to this. If we treat students well, if we make them feel that they are in an educational partnership with us, if we give them the courses they need to graduate and make our costs affordable, they will come to our schools.

Many of my colleagues may reject this simplistic approach to a facet of college administration that affects everyone in the academic community. Clearly, if we do not have students, we do not have an educational enterprise. Some may reject my basic premise that we need more practical and less theoretical approaches to enrolling and retaining students. I have tried to follow Friedrich Engels' adage, "An ounce of action is worth a ton of theory."

I know of several schools with intricate and sophisticated enrollment projection models and with very complicated theories as to why students leave their schools. Projection models and retention theories alone won't change a school's enrollment and retention problems. Let's get back to the basics. Let's listen to our students. Let's treat our students as valued customers. Let's have the courage to change what really needs to change in our offices, in our attitudes, in our processes, in our rules and regulations. Let's look ahead instead of relying on the way it has always been done. In short, let's change.

The purpose of this book is to describe a step-by-step practical and systematic approach to designing and implementing an enrollment and retention management program for colleges and universities. The book will focus on presenting a basic system for integrating the functions of the offices of enrollment management, retention management, admission, financial aid, registration, research and public relations, including publications and advertising. In addition, the book will illustrate how retention activities can support and enhance a school's marketing, recruitment and enrollment management programs. A simplified and basic approach will be given to explain the following.

1. The basic organizational structures necessary to implement successful enrollment and retention management programs
2. The role of research in developing enrollment and retention management programs
3. The necessary synergy between admission objectives and financial aid policies to achieve enrollment objectives
4. How to conduct marketing audits
5. How telecounseling can help to focus admission programs
6. The changing role of publications
7. The role of advertising in recruitment
8. The role of the president, faculty, and the entire campus community in enrollment and retention management
9. The role of financial aid in retention
10. The role of student debt in enrollment and retention
11. Problems common in developing enrollment and retention management programs
12. Staff development
13. The role of change in developing and implementing effective enrollment and retention management programs
14. Program evaluations
15. The future of enrollment and retention management programs

Few publications on the subject of enrollment and retention management combine the two processes or present retention management as a primary component of enrollment management. This is the approach I have taken because it has been effective at Suffolk University. Combining the two programs is an integral and frequent theme throughout this book. I believe that a school's enrollment management program will not be successful in meeting its objectives without a retention management program which supports and enhances those goals. Consider this: each year we enroll only 25% of our student population; retaining students makes up the other 75%. It's fiscal insanity to focus on expensive recruitment programs only to have students leave after six months or a year. I think it is safe to say that at most colleges and universities, these two functions are not integrated. Furthermore, I don't think colleges and universities pay enough attention to retention management.

I have attempted to present information in a practical, not a theoretical, way. It is my belief, based on the seminars and workshops I have attended, that university administrators want basic advice on how to implement a synergistic enrollment and retention management program at their campuses. While not every suggestion offered in this book will work at all schools, there are some that could work at most schools. No "cookie-cutter" approach will do. The only thing we can be certain of in developing enrollment and retention management programs is that they will and should be works in progress, with the only constant being the need to recognize, appreciate, and embrace change.

1

What Is Enrollment Management?

"Vision is the art of seeing things invisible."

— Jonathan Swift

There are almost as many definitions of enrollment management as there are schools that have enrollment management programs. Over the years my own definition of enrollment management has changed significantly. I realize that I have modified what I used to think of as enrollment management, or managing the enrollment of the entering freshman class, to a more fluid and global concept, involving the entire campus community. I have attempted to change the way I spend my time; moving away from simply analyzing freshmen applications and yield rates to planning strategically to meet the future enrollment needs of the university. Anticipating the changes that are likely to occur in higher education over the next five years and articulating those changes to the president, trustees, faculty, and the enrollment and retention management staff now constitutes the most important part of my work day. Planning to effectively incorporate distance learning options, corporate outreach programs, national and international collaborations, joint degree programs and affiliations with local area schools are intrinsic to my current concept of what enrollment management is and should be.

Enrollment management is forecasting trends that will likely affect higher education and using effective research to effectively plan for the future. Essential to any efficient enrollment management program is continuous assessment of policies and practices and articulating needed changes to the entire campus community. You really can't have an enrollment management program without listening to your student-customers and learning from them why they enrolled at your school and what are their perceptions of what it is your school does best.

Enrollment management is not a bag of tricks or a series of quick fixes. It does not hold only one administrator responsible for a school's enrollment success or failure. It does not ignore the campus culture or the faculty.

However You Define It, Enrollment Management Is . . .

1. Knowing what makes a student enroll at a school
2. Understanding the relationship of the student who enrolls with the student who withdraws and the student who persists
3. Knowing how students pay for their education
4. Strategically preparing to meet the future enrollment and financial needs of a school
5. Linking enrollment management with retention management

Essential Questions That Should Be Asked and Answered by Enrollment Management

1. What enrollment problems has the school had in the past?
2. How did the school respond to the problems?
3. What was the result?
4. What are the current pressing enrollment problems?
5. What is the school's current competitive edge? What will that edge be in five years?
6. What is the projected enrollment situation likely to be?
7. What external factors will affect enrollment?
8. Do enrollment projections match the necessary financial needs?
9. What systems are in place to offset declining enrollments?
10. What processes have been effective in increasing enrollment and why?
11. What processes have failed to increase enrollment and why?
12. How often are the processes analyzed and how quickly can the systems be changed to respond to enrollment needs and market opportunities?
13. What part does enrollment management play in retention management?
14. What is the school's retention and attrition rates?
15. What is the profile of the stop-out?
16. What is the profile of the persister?
17. What role do the president and academic deans play in enrollment management?
18. Do the academic programs complement the enrollment management objectives?

19. What role does enrollment management have in the budget process and in setting the institutional financial aid budget?
20. Is there sufficient research and data analyses to support enrollment management initiatives?
21. What role does the school's public relations program have in enrollment management?
22. What processes are in place to streamline operations, control costs and reduce expenses?
23. Is there understanding and support for the enrollment management program by senior staff and faculty?
24. Does the dean of enrollment management report either to the president, provost or academic vice-president?
25. Is the school poised to respond to change?

WHERE TO BEGIN

To effectively develop a division of enrollment management, a coordinated system—one that cuts across the traditional boundaries of specific job and office functions—is necessary. Institutional strategy, not one or two specific activities, is needed to ensure the success of the program. The way a school organizes its enrollment management office or division will depend upon the size of the school and whether the school is public or private, the history of the school and the magnitude of the enrollment problem. The culture of the institution as well as the school's "personality" must also be taken into account. The level of presidential support and the reporting structure will also influence how enrollment management is organized and implemented.

Over the years I have observed several institutions which were unable to effectively implement successful enrollment and retention management programs. Most of these schools shared one or more of the following pitfalls.

1. Not knowing or understanding the product
2. Not having access to good data and research
3. Not matching the enrollment management design with the "personality" of the institution
4. Not obtaining sufficient presidential support and commitment
5. Not giving the program enough time to develop and trying to do it all at once
6. Little or no coordination between the academic programs and the enrollment management program
7. Little or no coordination with the retention management program
8. Little or no integration with the financial aid program
9. Not articulating the strategy behind the program to the appropriate campus constituencies
10. Not including the right staff people in designing the program
11. Little or no staff development

12. Holding the enrollment manager solely responsible for the success or failure of the enrollment management program
13. Failing to make sure everyone involved understands the need for change
14. Failing to assess and evaluate all essential elements of the program
15. Taking the job too seriously and really believing one person can do it all

STAFFING

Just as there are several ways to design an enrollment management program, there are also many different reporting structures. What works at one school may not work at another. Program design and staffing will depend on the history of the school and the nature of the enrollment problem. In the enrollment management division at Suffolk University, I have found the following reporting structure effective:

1. Associate Dean of Enrollment and Retention Management
2. Director of Undergraduate Admission
3. Director of Graduate Admission
4. Director of Financial Aid
5. Registrar
6. Director of Enrollment Research
7. Director of International Programs
8. Director of Continuing Education and Corporate Outreach
9. Director of Publications and Advertising

I have read many articles about establishing a division of enrollment management that includes the student services function of the school. I see the value to such a structure, and at many schools it may be a recommended one. However, this would not work at many universities. Theoretically, including student services may be a preferred method of conducting enrollment management, but in practical terms, if it won't work at your school, don't insist on including that part of the school's administrative structure into a division of enrollment management.

REPORTS

The following is a list of reports that should be expected from the Division of Enrollment Management:

1. Enrollment in each student cohort
2. Retention in each student cohort compared with enrollment
3. Financial aid program and its impact on enrollment
4. International recruitment program
5. Telecounseling program and its impact on enrollment
6. National and international educational collaborations

7. Minority outreach program
8. Publications program and its impact on enrollment
9. Advertising program and its impact on enrollment
10. Direct mail program and its impact on enrollment
11. Alumni recruitment program
12. Analysis of research reports on new markets
13. Corporate outreach and continuing education programs and the impact on enrollment
14. Analysis of the synergy between the school's enrollment management objectives and retention management goals
15. Analysis of the school's enrollment management program in meeting the overall strategic plan for the college or university

Enrollment management is both a science and an art. However, in order to be successful, the program must be lead by a dynamic and confident individual with a great deal of creativity—someone who is a risk-taker and who realizes that success can only come through the people implementing the program. Efficient enrollment management programs are not built on systems but rather on people. The best research and organizational plan cannot compensate for a poorly trained or non-motivated staff. In addition, enrollment management must have the understanding and support from the president on down. Everyone must have some ownership of the program if it is to be effective. No one person can or should be responsible for the school's entire enrollment success or failure. Enrollment management, at its best, cuts across institutional lines, and demands that turf battles be kept to a minimum. It asks that everyone check their egos at the door. Enrollment management requires that the needs of students be placed above individual needs.

There are many ways to structure a division or department of enrollment management. On the following page is the organizational chart for the Division of Enrollment Management at Suffolk University. It is not the only way to organize a division of enrollment management. It is the one which best suited the needs of our students and the culture of our school.

ENROLLMENT MANAGEMENT DIVISION

Organization Chart

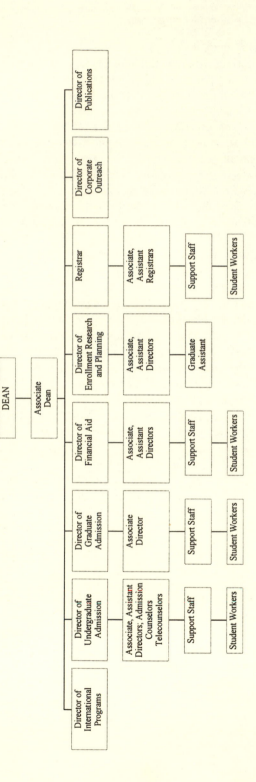

2

Who Is an Enrollment Manager?

"The duty of a dean is to make the college what the president has long as-
serted it already is."

— Henry Wriston

The overall responsibility of enrollment managers is to contribute to the fulfill-
ment of the mission of the college or university, to provide support services to
students through the admission, financial aid and registration processes, and to
serve as a resource to other campus constituencies, including faculty. Enrollment managers should also work synergistically with the dean of retention management.

Enrollment managers should be able to provide for the effective and efficient
integration of the admission, financial aid and registration functions with the
academic and student service functions. For an enrollment management program to be successful, the program's message must be articulated to the rest of
the campus community. Institutional strategy and collaboration is critical. The
marketing, research, recruitment, admission, financial aid and registration processes are a reflection and by-product of institutional support. They should complement the academic, political, administrative, and managerial environment of
the college or university. It is the responsibility of enrollment managers to involve and educate members of the school community about the long-term purposes and goals of the enrollment management program and to seek advice and

support from as many campus constituencies as is necessary to achieve those goals.

Enrollment managers should be thinking, searching, and creative people who have a commitment to curiosity, an expectation of excellence, and a humanistic approach to problem solving. They should be effective leaders who are willing to analyze problems, suggest solutions, and use change advantageously. Enrollment managers should blend the pragmatic with the philosophical concerns of the schools they serve. They should be able to communicate these concerns to the appropriate members of the academic and administrative community.

Charisma is a difficult quality to define. A charismatic person knows how to react to a wide range of situations and people and knows how to get people to change their behavior without intimidation or fear. Enrollment managers, by the very nature of the work they do, are asking people to change and are suggesting that systems change. This puts enormous pressure on the campus culture, and on staff, some of whom may be determined to maintain the status quo. Having the ability to gently move people and systems, while at the same time being tough enough to weather turf battles and intractable employees, is essential to an enrollment manager's success. It is also important that enrollment managers have a working knowledge of the admission, financial aid, and registration processes and have an appreciation of the data analysis and research techniques necessary to ask the right questions and to implement effective and efficient changes.

If I Were Conducting a Search for a Dean of Enrollment Management, I Would Look for a Candidate Who . . .

1. Has at least ten years of experience in higher education administration and has a clear understanding of marketing principles, recruitment and admission processes, financial aid, registration, international collaborations, corporate outreach, advertising and publications
2. Is able to balance the big picture with detail and knows the right questions to ask
3. Is future oriented and can articulate a vision about the direction of enrollment management programs in the future, including the role of distance learning and campus mergers and affiliations
4. Is goal oriented and can set priorities and remain focused
5. Can manage time well
6. Can demonstrate the ability to plan rather than to react to situations and can concentrate on making a few good decisions
7. Can demonstrate political astuteness and a tolerance and respect for the campus culture
8. Has the ability to build coalitions
9. Has good communication and writing skills
10. Has the ability to be flexible

11. Is a team player who can build on the strengths of people and effectively deal with their shortcomings
12. Has the ability to listen, *really* listen to people
13. Is able to work long hours and travel whenever necessary
14. Enjoys good health
15. Knows how to set limits and recognizes that an effective enrollment management program should always be a work in progress
16. Is secure enough to take risks and convert opportunities into positive results
17. Has a good sense of humor
18. Has learned how to say no
19. Is trustworthy
20. Is a change agent

If I Were Conducting a Search for a Dean of Enrollment Management, I Would Not Select Someone with the Following Characteristics

1. Has less than ten years of experience in higher education administration
2. Has experience only in undergraduate admission
3. Has no experience in the financial aid or registration processes
4. Left their last job after fewer than three years in the position
5. Speaks negatively about people from his/her last job
6. Exhibits workaholic tendencies
7. Shows signs of stress or burnout
8. Is afraid of making mistakes
9. Is fearful or angry
10. Does not smile

We really are looking for an administrative "super star," someone with a creative mind, and an expert's knowledge, a futurist, someone who has the ability to deal calmly in a crisis, who has good public relations skills, and who has the courage to make tough decisions and persevere. This is a lot to expect from any one person. I have known dedicated and talented enrollment managers who had excellent administrative skills but who suffered from classic burn-out. The nature and scope of the job create a climate that asks for more and better each year. Unless you have a clear sense of self and an inherent belief that problems can and will be solved, it is difficult to be effective. Unless you are willing to take a vacation or spend time with family or friends, you can't be effective. Unless you know or learn how to relax, you won't be effective. Unless you recognize that working longer is not as beneficial as working smarter, you won't be effective. Unless you come to realize that you have only one body and as time moves on, it requires at least some of your attention, you may not be as effective as someone working with both a healthy mind and body. Enrollment management is both a profession and a personal reflection of oneself. Keeping the job in perspective and enjoying a personal and family life are as important as next year's entering class. In short, be good to yourself and to those around you.

Enrollment managers should devote at least one day a week to research. Schedule your week to allow for quiet time. For most of my professional life, I have spent one day a week either at home or in the library, conducting research and trying to solve problems which were impossible to solve in the office. None of my superiors ever objected to this arrangement. Some of the best and most innovative parts of the enrollment management programs I helped to create came from these days spent in "splendid isolation."

The following are some of the publications enrollment managers should be reading weekly, monthly, and quarterly:

Enrollment and Retention

Academe
Academic Advising News
American Association for Higher Education Bulletin
Change
The College Board News
The College Board Review
College and University
College Student Journal
Currents
Distance Education Report
Higher Education and National Affairs
Journal of College Admission
Journal of College Student Development
Journal of Counseling and Development
Journal for Higher Education Management
Journal of Marketing for Higher Education
The Magazine of the Graduate Management Admissions Council
The MBA Newsletter
National Academic Advising Association Journal
National Academic Student Personnel Journal
Occupational Outlook Quarterly
Planning for Higher Education
Private Colleges and Universities
Recruitment and Retention in Higher Education
The Review of Higher Education
Strategies
Student Poll

Adult/Continuing Education

Adult Education
Adult Learning
School-to-Work Report

Financial Aid/Finance

Business Officer
Financial Aid Transcript
Funding Alert
Journal of Student Financial Aid
Postsecondary Education Opportunity
Solutions
Student Aid News

International

Advising Quarterly
The Economist
Educational Associate
International Educator
International Schools Journal
World Education & News Reviews

Marketing

Admissions Marketing Report
American Marketing Association Newsletter
The Education Investor
Journal of Marketing
Journal of Marketing Education
Marketing Higher Education Newsletter
Telemarketing

Research

Higher Education Abstracts
Journal of Advertising Research
Journal of Consumer Affairs
Journal of Consumer Behavior
Journal of Marketing Research
Planning for Higher Education
Research in Higher Education
The Review of Higher Education

Human Resources

Issues and Observations
Women in Higher Education
Working Smart, Executive Strategies

Magazines

American Demographics
Change
The Futurist

Weekly Newspapers/Newsletters

The Chronicle of Higher Education
The Kiplinger Washington Newsletter

Daily Newspapers

Local newspaper
The Christian Science Monitor
The New York Times
USA Today
The Wall Street Journal
World Wide Web Sites

There are advanced degrees in higher education administration which specialize in enrollment management. While theoretical knowledge is important, it cannot replace experience. A seasoned enrollment manager cannot be manufactured in the classroom or from a textbook. Enrollment management requires talented and energetic administrators with years of firsthand experience. Enrollment managers must be able to bring out the best in their staffs, to focus on people's strengths, to rise above the campus' politics and to never forget to smile.

3

The Future of
Enrollment Management

"I have been over into the future, and it works."

—Lincoln Steffens

Just when you think you have organized and implemented the best enrollment management program possible, it will be time to change it. Over the years, I have divided my time between undergraduate and graduate enrollment management activities. I realize now that doing just this will be neither sufficient nor relevant in the future. Once again, *change*, our constant companion, dictates that we look at the way we do business with an eye on the envisioned future.

Over the Next Few Years, I Expect Enrollment Management Programs Will Expand to Include the Following

1. Corporate outreach programs
2. Distance learning programs
3. Combined degree programs
4. Collaborations with local colleges and universities
5. International contracts and collaborations

There can be several other new and innovative ways to diversify the student population and increase revenue. The following are examples of a few suggestions.

CORPORATE OUTREACH ACTIVITIES

According to the Carnegie Foundation, an estimated $100 billion is being spent by corporations to train and retrain their employees. Corporations have established nearly 20 degree-granting institutions, and the trend is to continue to increase corporate educational opportunities and course offerings. Motorola has a university with hundreds of instructors and hopes in the future to ensure that every employee takes one month of training every year. Chaparral Steel has a policy to keep 85% of its employees enrolled in some training program. The list goes on and this trend is likely to increase, not decrease, in the future.

Regardless of their size or location, all colleges and universities should be reaching out to local companies and corporations and forging educational alliances with them. This is one way to provide employees with the technological or remedial training they need and want and one way for the college or university to increase enrollment and revenue. There are several ways to conduct this type of activity. I will describe what we did at Suffolk University, since in a relatively short period of time our corporate outreach activities have been successful.

First, we hired a part-time director of contract training and education who worked out of the office of enrollment management and reported to the dean. Monies were allocated and a marketing plan was written and approved by the dean of enrollment management and the academic deans. An understanding was reached that if the program was successful and began to generate income, the position would be increased to full-time. (This was done in six months.)

Second, we asked the director to meet with faculty and with the academic deans and department chairpersons to learn of any corporate contacts they had, to ascertain who would be interested in teaching corporate clients in off-site locations and to obtain suggestions for courses and seminars.

Third, the director of corporate outreach met with the dean of enrollment and with the director of publications. A corporate portfolio was designed listing what courses and programs are currently offered, what certificate programs are available, and what courses and training programs could be offered in the future.

Course Offerings Included

- Conflict Resolution
- Media Relations
- Change Management
- Decision-Making
- International Marketing

- Diversity
- Professional Development

Sample Training Areas Included

- Doing Business in the Global Environment
- Entrepreneurial Management
- International Economics
- Financial Planning and Corporate Finance
- Mergers and Acquisitions
- Strategic Marketing
- ISO 9000
- Presentation Skills

Fourth, the director set up appointments with the appropriate person in each company she visited. She met with the key people and she listened. She learned that few companies want "canned" programs. Rather, they are looking for customized courses that relate specifically to the needs of their organization and employees. Companies want tailored programs leading to professional certification, academic credits, or undergraduate and graduate degrees. Managers want programs that can help give their employees the tools necessary to compete in the workplace of the future. They want faculty who can design courses that are practical, relevant, and future-oriented. They want programs taught in a convenient location and at a convenient time. A school that can respond in a timely and non-bureaucratic way to meeting the needs of the corporate client will be successful in signing contracts. A school that can incorporate enrollment management principles into its corporate contract training program will both increase revenues and enrollment for the school and diversify its student body.

Employees can no longer expect to stay in the same job or in the same field for their entire working lives. New and different skills will be required to keep employees current and corporations competitive. As the needs of the work force change, new opportunities for the enrollment of non-traditional students will increase. Corporate training opportunities can lead to the expansion of traditional student markets and create a win-win situation for everyone.

DISTANCE LEARNING PROGRAMS

In the past 25 years there has been an explosion in creating alternative ways of delivering educational services. Currently, there is a mix of distance learning and teleconferencing networks throughout the world. Regardless of the name used, the concept is the same: taking courses or earning a degree without physically visiting the campus. Distance learning programs are projected to increase in the years ahead. These programs are designed to meet the needs of people who need or want continuous training and who have irregular working hours or other commitments that make taking courses in the traditional way difficult or impossible. Distance learning techniques make it possible to offer courses and seminars throughout the world from the home campus.

According to the Council for Distance Learning, as many as 10 million people worldwide study off-campus each year, learning through cable television, satellite, or guided independent study programs. Statistics show that 6% of all college credits earned in the United States today are earned electronically. Recently, trustees of the University of Maine voted to convert a distance learning network into a degree granting institution. The network is a system of voice, video, and computer links through which students in off-campus locations can take credit and non-credit courses.

Beginning this year students will have an opportunity to enroll in the Western Governors Association's University. Using the Internet, e-mail, CD-ROMs, interactive video networks, television, cable, and a satellite system, the WGU will offer courses from dozens of Western colleges and universities. WGU will also provide certification and job training for companies. This ambitious virtual learning experience could change the entire way American education is delivered in the future.

The University of Phoenix has an On-line Campus which allows students to attend classes 24 hours a day, seven days a week, from anywhere in the world. I recently received a brochure explaining this program and I live in Massachusetts! IBM has a wonderful series of television ads that explain how their system allows students to study anything, anytime, anywhere. I particularly like the commercial that shows an Italian farmer speaking with his granddaughter and explaining to her how he just earned his doctoral degree from the University of Indiana. It's a powerful and engaging advertisement and for enrollment managers, it carries a poignant message about the future of educational delivery systems.

Let's take a look at some of the programs currently being offered by colleges and universities around the country.

George Washington University offers an on-line master's degree program in educational technology leadership. Students can watch lectures on satellite television, send papers through an electronic bulletin board, and talk to their professors via e-mail.

The University of Massachusetts at Dartmouth recently began an on-line course in writing for the World Wide Web.

New York University's Information Technologies Institute offers a 16 credit graduate entirely through an interactive network.

Colorado's National Technical University consists of 94 engineering colleges sending courses directly to workplaces.

Pennsylvania State University has over 18,000 students enrolled in distance learning programs.

Georgetown University's Center for International Business Education and Research is offering the first of its kind in satellite long-distance education centers for international business and trade. This project is funded by NASA and the Inter-American Development Bank.

Distance learning options allow people to work at their own pace and in their own home or work environment. In the future, telecommunications will be a standard collegiate practice and the interactive video disc will be a powerful teaching tool. Satellite broadcasts, fiber-optic networks, e-mail and bulletin boards, interactive television and the Internet will revolutionize higher education. New technologies present both challenges and opportunities for the enrollment management program of the future. This new technology will not disappear or self-destruct. There is no turning back. While it is unlikely that distance learning programs will replace the traditional campus, enrollment management programs and enrollment managers must begin *today* to expand their horizons to incorporate these new methods of educational delivery and to make technology work for them.

COMBINED DEGREE PROGRAMS

As corporate America becomes leaner and companies continue to downsize, employees are looking for new ways to make themselves more competitive and attractive to their companies. One way to do this is to continue their education, to re-train, to specialize. This training could involve studying in a combined degree program, or earning a second degree.

Over the past five years we have seen a proliferation of combined degree programs at Suffolk University. We have listened as our student-customers told us the type of programs they want. We have a well-established and respected law school. Our students told us that what they wanted were combined graduate school and law school programs. We currently offer combined degrees in:

- Juris Doctor and Master of Business Administration—JD/MBA
- Juris Doctor and Master of Public Administration—JD/MPA
- Juris Doctor and Master of International Economics—JD/MSIE
- Juris Doctor and Master of Science in Finance—JD/MSF

These joint degree programs prepare graduates to compete for jobs in the legal, business, public management, financial, and international economics fields. In addition, graduates of the dual degree programs have added flexibility to transition easily between careers requiring specialization.

Enrollment in these combined degree programs continue to increase each year. Offering dual degrees has allowed Suffolk University to tap into new student markets and has contributed to expanding the role of the enrollment management division. It has forced us to think about what program options our current students want as well as to prepare for the students of tomorrow. It has enabled the University to strategically link the Law School and graduate school departments and has forged new and vital relationships between the deans and faculty of the two schools.

COLLABORATIONS WITH LOCAL COLLEGES AND UNIVERSITIES

Over the past decade, several colleges have merged, consolidated, or offered joint degree programs with neighboring institutions. I see this type of cooperation between schools as another way for enrollment managers to do business in the future. This type of collaboration allows both schools to be in a win-win situation. They can offer programs which, if offered alone, might be too expensive. It also brings the faculty of both schools together and reduces the costs for advertising, publications, and other types of public relations.

To initiate this process, a senior official from one school has to contact the appropriate person at the other school to determine whether an interest in collaborating exists. If so, the next step is to involve the academic deans to determine what courses or programs could be offered jointly. Then the deans of enrollment management at each school must decide how to market the program. This is another way for the enrollment management program to increase student enrollment, increase tuition revenues, expand course offerings and engage the constituencies of both campuses in a new educational venture.

INTERNATIONAL COLLABORATIONS

I remember sitting in a restaurant in Amsterdam and looking around at the people using their cellular phones, engaged in animated conversation, presumably closing a "big deal." I also remember thinking that I had just signed an agreement with an international organization to offer one of our educational programs in-country. The contract was worth a great deal of money and took a long time to negotiate. I further recall thinking that the work I was doing was not dissimilar to what all the other business people in that Amsterdam restaurant were doing. Higher education is a big business. It's an export business. In many parts of the world, although not all, America's higher education system is still the preferred model. I do not know for certain how long this will last, but for now I know that I must devote a portion of my work week and a great deal of my energy to exporting our educational product. The work is often tedious (not glamorous) and requires a deep understanding of the people, culture, economy, educational system, and problems of the country. For Suffolk University, the result has been worth the effort. International collaborations now form a significant part of our budget. We are offering programs in several countries and have opened a satellite campus in Madrid. A week does not pass when we do not receive a request from a potential international educational partner. Distance learning options will make it easier and less costly to enter into joint collaborations with overseas partners. This is a trend I believe will continue in the future.

There are several ways to initiate this type of activity. At Suffolk we began by studying the needs of particular countries in which the University had strong ties or important contacts. If it seemed reasonable that there was a good "match" between what we could offer and what the country needed, someone from the enrollment management staff would travel and meet with the appropriate people and begin the negotiations. Lengthy discussions are usually part of this process. Occasionally, coming to a mutually agreeable solution seemed almost impossible. However, that was the exception. In most cases, we were able to reach a compromise that involved offering degree programs or courses incounty, offering courses via distance learning, or arranging seminars for international students and businessmen at our Boston campus.

The work can often be fun and exciting. It is frequently demanding. It is always different. This type of activity allows the enrollment manager to expand where and to whom courses are offered. It diversifies the campus by enrolling students with varied backgrounds. And no one complains about the additional revenue!

As I mentioned in the beginning of this chapter, there are many other ways of expanding enrollment and changing and broadening the ways an enrollment manager does business. I listed these five because these are the new ways we have increased both students and revenue at Suffolk University. Though not as developed as other parts of our enrollment management program, I believe that within these five new areas lie our greatest source of expansion in the years to come. More *change*.

The pie chart on the following page illustrates how I expect enrollment management duties to change in the next few years.

DIVISION OF ENROLLMENT MANAGEMENT

1990 - 1995

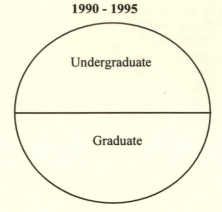

1995 - 2000

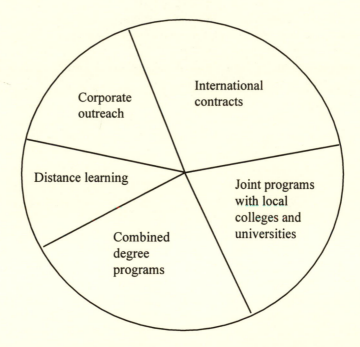

4

The Role of Research in Enrollment Management

"When offered different theories, start with the simplest one."

—Ockham's Razor

I am always amazed at the colleges and universities which have enrollment and retention management programs but do not have a researcher as part of the team. Not having a researcher in the divisions of enrollment and retention management is like driving a car without an engine. It is impossible to have an effective and efficient enrollment and retention management program without a research component, without the data to tell you who your student-clients are, what their needs are, and why they enroll in and remain at or leave your school. A researcher is not an "extra" staff member. The position is an essential one and the staff member should be carefully selected.

A researcher should be assigned to the office of enrollment management and should not be borrowed from institutional research or some other university department. Nor should this be an outsourced position. There is too much data that needs to be collected and analyzed to relegate this to a half-time position. It is essential that the researcher serve as a liaison with other offices, especially the fiscal office. Good research should be able to project enrollments and tuition revenues for each semester and provide critical input into the budget process. The researcher should be a part of the school's strategic planning committee or should at least be aware of the institution's strategic direction and planning.

Research needs should be prioritized, as there will probably be more requests than there is time in the day to accomplish them.

Components of an Effective Research Program

1. Obtain top-level commitment that this is an integral part of the enrollment and retention management programs. I would relinquish many other staff lines before this one.
2. Determine your school's specific enrollment and retention research needs. What information do you need and why? Prioritize.
3. Obtain research requests in writing, including goals and action to be taken based on the study's findings.
4. The researcher should be given the right to veto research requests that are unnecessary or a duplication of effort.
5. Determine which research mechanisms are most appropriate to use: mail surveys, focus groups, or telephone calls.
6. Allocate the personnel and financial resources necessary to achieve the desired results.
7. Define research goals in terms that can be measured.
8. The findings of research projects should be analyzed, evaluated, and presented to the deans of enrollment and retention management for implementation.
9. Research studies should be compared from one year to another and should be shared with all appropriate staff members.
10. The researcher should attend at least one seminar or conference per year to meet with people doing similar work. I have observed our researcher sitting day after day in front of his computer screen and wondered how he has kept his sanity. Colleagues can help.

SUGGESTED RESEARCH REPORTS

The following is a suggested list of reports that should be generated each year by the director of enrollment research.

Marketing and Enrollment

1. Demographic analysis of current and projected student markets
2. Geodemographic analysis of current and projected student markets
3. Enrollment forecasting
4. Monthly enrollment projection statistics for all student cohorts
5. New student enrollment projections
6. Comparison of projected and actual enrollments
7. Calculation of cost to recruit undergraduate and graduate students
8. Importance of factors in enrollment decision, including reputation, cost, class size, accessibility, faculty, and curriculum

9. Measurement of outreach activities for freshmen, transfer students, graduate students, adult learners, and corporate clients
10. Analysis of the effectiveness of direct mail program, college fairs, telecounseling, advertising, publications, and school visits
11. Enrollment Planning Service data analysis of the College Board
12. Admitted student questionnaires—undergraduate and graduate
13. Competitor analysis
14. Market share analysis
15. Comparative analysis of competitor institutions
16. Characteristics of students who enroll, including academic profile, income, gender, ethnicity, and geographic location
17. Characteristics of accepted students who did not enroll, including academic profile, income, gender, ethnicity, and geographic location
18. Orientation survey analysis
19. Survey by students of the admission, financial aid, registration, and bursar offices
20. Analysis of advertising, publications, and public relations campaigns

Financial Aid Analysis

1. Financial aid awards and enrollment yields
2. Admitted Student Questionnaire financial data analysis of the College Board including the percent of non-enrolling students not offered financial aid and the percent of non-enrolling students offered aid at competitor schools
3. Tuition pricing analysis
4. Income profile
5. Net tuition analysis
6. Tuition discounting and enrollment yields
7. Financial aid packaging analysis
8. Comparative tuition data
9. Part-time tuition pricing policies
10. Impact of tuition increases on enrollment and retention

Retention Reports

1. Retention statistics from fall to spring semester
2. Retention statistics from spring to fall semester
3. Attrition and retention rates for freshmen, sophomores, juniors, seniors, minority students, adult students, part-time students, athletes, international students, and graduate students
4. Attrition vs. enrollment, fall to spring semesters and spring to fall semesters
5. Attrition rates by academic profile, income, gender, ethnicity, commuter or residential status, and year in school

6. Persistence rates by academic profile, income, gender, ethnicity, commuter or residential status, and year in school
7. Attrition rates by major and program
8. Persistence rates by major and program
9. Cooperative Institutional Research Program (CIRP) freshmen analysis
10. Attrition rates of adult learners
11. Persistence rates of adult learners
12. Withdrawal survey analysis
13. Leave of absence and probation analysis
14. Graduation statistics
15. High-risk student data analysis

Surveys and Publications

1. College Board Undergraduate and Graduate Surveys
2. Barron's *Profiles*
3. Peterson's Undergraduate and Graduate Surveys
4. *Money* magazine Survey
5. *U.S. News & World Report* Survey
6. Orchard House Survey

Miscellaneous

1. Six-week survey of new freshmen and transfer students
2. Exit survey of graduating students
3. Economic impact of international students on the local economy
4. Alumni survey
5. Parent questionnaire
6. Publications focus-group analysis
7. Advertising focus-group analysis
8. Summer session course offering analysis
9. Salary statistics of graduates

Unless there is an administrator who will accept responsibility for the information gathered, and can act on and make decisions based on the data, all of the time and energy that went into the research will be wasted. Research is as valuable as it is understood and constructively used. Be prepared to implement necessary changes.

If you are just beginning to establish offices of enrollment and retention management, be certain to include a researcher as part of your team. If you already have a division of enrollment and retention management and don't have a researcher, hire one. If you have a division of enrollment and retention management and have a good researcher, give that person a raise!

5

Marketing

"Some problems are so difficult they can't be solved in a million years—unless someone thinks about them for five minutes."

— H. L. Mencken

Perhaps I am oversimplifying, but to me, higher education marketing is nothing more than offering the right academic programs and courses at the right time and place, and at the right price, to the right student markets. As simple as this sounds, anyone in higher education administration who has attempted to design and implement a marketing plan knows that this is one of the most difficult aspects of enrollment management.

I have been on the giving and receiving ends of writing marketing plans. I have written thoughtful, well-organized plans based on sound research only to see the plan sit on a shelf, the end product of a poorly planned implementation program. I have also participated in rushing through a plan based on inadequate analysis, the by-product of the plea to *do* something, anything, now. Neither approach is recommended.

There are a number of excellent publications dealing with the need for and the how-to of college marketing. Some strategies suggest such complicated research and enrollment projection formulas that it is impossible for even a well-organized enrollment management office to implement. Some colleges and universities go the route of hiring an outside consulting firm to design an overall enrollment strategy for them. I am not criticizing either approach. However, neither has worked for me.

  This chapter presents what may be considered a simplistic approach to college marketing. I would like to have this chapter reviewed as one offering practical suggestions on how to market colleges and universities. What I want to share with you is what I think marketing is and is not, and why it is difficult to implement sound marketing principles in college and university environments.

  College marketing is not a single plan, but a series of integrated plans. Marketing is not the sole responsibility of the admission office. That is the sales office, not the product design office. College marketing should not be equated with advertising, which is only a small part of the overall marketing plan nor with aggressive, slick or questionable recruitment techniques. College marketing is not about adding more staff to the admission office or hiring a public relations firm to create an institutional image. It is not an isolated campus activity nor a panacea for all of a school's problems.

College Marketing Should Be Based on These Considerations

1. A school's marketing strength should be based on the quality of its educational programs, the quality of its students and faculty, and a school's efforts to retain the students it admits.
2. A school's marketing program should be based on institutional and enrollment research and should answer the fundamental questions of why students enroll and why they leave. Research that is based on anyalytical reasoning and has carefully assessed the needs, perceptions, and attitudes of the target audiences, should form the basis of the marketing plan.
3. A school's marketing plan should be based on who the school currently enrolls and why.
4. A school's marketing program should include who the school wants to enroll and why.
5. A school's marketing program should have clearly articulated goals and strategies, and a reasonable time frame in which to accomplish these goals.
6. A school's marketing program should give consideration to developing new markets based on geographic, demographic, and psychographic information, and national trends. It should be consistent with the analysis of a school's institutional and enrollment research. Economics, technological advances, and political trends should also be taken into account when developing strategic marketing plans.
7. The development of new markets should be compatible with a school's enrollment objectives, resources, staffing decisions, and overall mission.
8. Separate marketing plans should be developed for each student market, including: undergraduate and graduate students, adult and part-time students, transfer students, male and female populations, international students, ESL students, honors students, commuter and residential students, financial aid recipients, corporate clients, and a continuing education population.

9. Information from focus groups of enrolled students, as well as students who chose not to enroll and students who left the institution, should be incorporated into an overall marketing plan.

10. A committee consisting of various campus constituencies, including representatives of the business office, development office, public relations, faculty, alumni office, and counseling and placement offices, should provide feedback to the dean of enrollment management and to the admission personnel on a school's marketing proposals.

11. A marketing audit should be conducted every three months to assess the effectiveness of each plan as well as to highlight problems. This allows the admission staff to change what is no longer working in their specific market, to strengthen those aspects of their plan that appear to be effective, and to share information with other staff members.

12. It is the responsibility of the dean or vice president of enrollment management to inform and educate members of the college or university community of the outcome of all marketing plans.

13. A school's marketing program should concentrate on producing a few, well-targeted results. A good marketing program is the product of thoughtful analysis, imagination, and judgment.

14. A school's marketing plans will be successful only if the right people are used to write and implement the program and one person is held accountable.

15. Marketing in higher education should be an evolutionary process and one of continuous improvement. Don't expect miracles overnight.

WHY IS MARKETING IN HIGHER EDUCATION SO DIFFICULT?

Marketing a college education is not the same as selling a bar of soap. The latter is tangible, the former is not. Implicit in higher education marketing is the *hope* that a college degree will result in a "better life" or at least a better paying job. But you cannot see or feel a college degree and there is no *guarantee* that you will get a better paying job or any job after four years of college. There is increased public skepticism that a college education costs too much, and may result in many young people mortgaging their futures by borrowing too much, and that the outcome in general may not be worth the time and effort.

Higher education is not by tradition or inclination a market-driven industry. Only in the last 15 to 20 years has there been a serious discussion and incorporation of basic marketing principles into college admission programs. For a long time, marketing was considered by many in academic circles, as an undignified and inappropriate endeavor for a college or university. Some faculty still maintain this position.

Product differentiation or what makes one school different from another, is difficult to assess. However, it is the differences, not the similarities, that should form the basis of a good marketing plan. This is essential in creating a school's special market niche. For too long, admission recruitment programs reflected what every other school was doing and did not focus on what their school offered and how it *differed* from its competitors. Consider the college viewbook. Many look the same: glossy pictures, smiling faces, but little or nothing in the book about what makes this school *different*. Of course in order to project differences, you really must have a program or something which your school does better than any other school. You can only sell or market what is available on your campus. You cannot fabricate uniqueness. Your school either has something special or different to market or it doesn't.

In most college and university hierarchies, it is difficult for one person to have the authority over all aspects of the marketing process. Often, authority and control for this process rests with several people. That is a fundamental difference from marketing in industry. There, authority for the marketing process usually rests with one person or a small group of people. The fact that the marketing authority in higher education is often a shared responsibility with many people, makes it a less efficient function.

A lack of effective market research dooms many marketing plans to failure. I don't know how any school can have a marketing plan that is not based on valid and current research or does not reflect the opinions of its prospective and enrolled students. Yet I believe that many schools do not include their researcher (if they have one) as part of the marketing planning process. Marketing plans usually begin and end in the admission office, often with little input from other administrative constituencies.

Many higher education administrators consider the success or failure of meeting enrollment goals as the failure or success of the admission office alone. That office is the sales office and it can only market to potential students what the school has to offer: its academic programs, its faculty, and its graduate profile. No marketing plan can make up for what the school does not have to offer or does not do well.

Some marketing strategies may ask for changes in the curriculum, or for changes when certain courses are taught. Marketing suggestions may affect the "academic side of the house." Faculty often regard their programs and their departments as immune to any marketing analysis or plan. Yet what courses are taught, what programs are offered, and when they are offered may be some of the reasons for enrollment declines.

Some marketing plans fail because the necessary financial resources or personnel are not committed to make the plan succeed. Some marketing plans fail because the wrong people are assigned to implement the plans. Some marketing plans fail because there is no effective evaluation process and no clear set of goals, objectives, and strategies.

HOW TO DEVELOP A SIMPLE MARKETING PLAN

There are several excellent publications and seminars that outline in detail how to write and implement effective marketing plans. The following are some practical suggestions.

1. Conduct the *research* necessary to develop an effective plan. Determine what are your school's strengths and weaknesses. What is it that you do well? What don't you do well? Consider your preferred class profile and why that profile is desired. Compare that profile with the profile of currently enrolled students. Know everything there is to know about your primary, secondary, and tertiary markets. Analyze the effectiveness of your recruitment and promotional materials by asking your student-clients about them. Listen to what your current students tell you are your school's distinctive features.

2. After this information is gathered and analyzed, the dean of enrollment management has the challenge of assigning the appropriate *personnel* and allocating the necessary *financial* resources needed to make the plan succeed.

3. Conduct effective *competitive analysis*. Who are your competitors? Who would you like them to be? What do you do better than your competitors? Worse? Why? Do you really have something different to market to potential students?

4. Determine exactly what your *product* is. In terms of your curricula, what is offered and when is it offered? Is it consistent with the mission of the school and the needs of your students? Have you considered the companies in your area and the employment and retraining needs of your adult learners? Do you listen to the corporate leaders in your community about what kinds of skills are needed in their workers? Can you enter into a partnership with area businesses to supply them with the employees they need and want? What do your graduates say about your "product"? Did the education they received at your school prepare them for the world of work? If yes, how? Is that the message conveyed to prospective students and their families? All messages should be consistent.

5. What about your *price*? How does it compare with other schools and with your main competitor institutions? Is your price consistent with your positioning? Is the family income of the majority of your students compatible with tuition costs? Are most of your students leaving because they cannot afford to stay? If that is the case, what can be done? Does the dean or vice president of enrollment management have an opportunity to present this information to senior management? I know of one school who was enrolling a freshmen class that research indicated came from families whose incomes were not a good match with the tuition charged at the school. The dean of enrollment management was able to prove that 25% of the freshmen class withdrew because of financial reasons. Students liked the school, the faculty, and the courses. They simply could not afford to attend. Something had to be done and it was. This university increased the amount of institutional funding. The directors of admission and financial aid met with the dean of enrollment management and the budget officer to determine how to best meet the net tuition needs of the university and how to match those needs with the marketing and recruitment programs. Admission counselors

were informed to adjust their recruitment activities accordingly and to increase their activities with specific cohorts of prospects. The deans of enrollment and retention management met and outlined the parameters for advising students to drop from full-time to part-time status in order to meet
their financial obligations. The dean of enrollment management met with
the vice president for development to plan strategies for how to obtain
scholarship funding from potential donors. A case statement was written,
outlining the need for scholarships. Finally, the dean of enrollment management met with the president and treasurer and obtained their approval
with regard to the maximum tuition discount. These decisions resulted, in
the first year, in fewer freshmen but greater net tuition revenues.

6. How do you *promote* your school? How effective is your direct mail pro-
    gram and materials, and your participation in high school visits and college
    fairs? How do you measure the effectiveness or ineffectiveness of your
    school's recruitment plans? How often do you measure your outreach ac-
    tivities? Is your school's advertising, radio, television, and public relations
    campaign consistent with your institution's image? More important, does
    that image represent reality? Are the letters, catalogs, and all other printed
    promotional materials sent to prospective students consistent with the other
    parts of your promotional plans? Remember, perception becomes reality.
    To be effective, all aspects of your promotional program should comple-
    ment each other and all should be consistent.

7. *Where* are your programs offered? Is the location convenient for your popu-
    lation? Is your school accessible to public transportation? Is parking con-
    venient and adequate? What about off-site locations? Does research indi-
    cate that you should offer courses and some programs at a satellite campus?
    (Will distance learning technology make all of these moot questions in the
    future?)

8. How is your product *distributed*? How does your marketing message reach
    potential markets? Did you allocate sufficient resources and personnel in
    developing the plans? What has succeeded or failed? Why?

9. How do you *evaluate* your plan and determine benchmarks? How do you
    set targets? How do you establish your one, three, and five year goals?

10. How do you *change* your plan if it needs changing? What processes are in
    place to change what is not working and to strengthen what is? What re-
    sources can be allocated to strengthen the parts of the program which need
    to be strengthened? What resources can be added to support the weaker
    parts of the marketing plan?

I have used the suggestions listed above as a blueprint for writing and implementing marketing plans. Of course this process can be made much more
complicated. However, it doesn't need to be. Keep it simple. Implement, and
change, when necessary.

6

Telecounseling: Pick Up the Phone

"Reach out and touch someone."

—AT&T slogan

Whatever you wish to call it—telemarketing, telecounseling, or telequalifying—
someone in the offices of enrollment and retention management should be contacting prospective applicants or currently enrolled students by telephone. Often
colleges and universities use the phone in the undergraduate admission program
in an attempt to prompt uncommitted applicants to proceed to the next strategic
point in the enrollment decision process. I have taken a somewhat broader approach to using the phone and define telecounseling in the following way.

Telecounseling is the process of establishing contact and a relationship with
either a prospective or currently enrolled student for the purpose of assisting the
undergraduate, graduate, adult, or non-traditional student with meeting their
enrollment, registration, financial aid, and retention objectives. Telecounseling
can also be used in corporate outreach activities and with parents and alumni
groups.

Telecounseling is an ongoing, flexible, and computer-assisted process involving trained personnel, and student workers. Telecounseling is an effective vehicle to conduct research and evaluate a school's enrollment and retention management programs.

The following are examples of the applicant and enrolled student cohorts who should be contacted in a telecounseling program.

- Prospective freshmen
- Families of prospective students
- Prospective transfer students
- Prospective graduate students
- Prospective adult and non-traditional students
- Prospective corporate clients
- Accepted applicants who have not applied for financial aid
- Accepted, deposited applicants who have not applied for financial aid
- Accepted, deposited undergraduate and graduate students who did not   register
- Accepted, deposited applicants who did not attend orientation
- Accepted undergraduate and graduate students who did not enroll
- Fall semester students who did not pre-register for the spring semester
- Spring semester students who have not pre-registered for the fall semester
- Students who have taken a leave of absence
- Students with unpaid tuition balances
- Summer phone calls to first semester sophomores
- Families of prospective and enrolled students
- Alumni groups and organizations

Before a program can be initiated, a clear sense of the purpose of the phone calls must be established. Scripts should be written and the appropriate staff trained in how to conduct the telephone session. What is said, how it is said, and how staff is trained will depend on the individual college or university. One person who is essential in any telecounseling program is the director of research. This person can guide the telecounseling staff to ask the most appropriate questions and prepare relevant reports. It is important that all telecounselors report the results of their phone conversations to the appropriate staff members, including the directors of undergraduate and graduate admission and the deans of enrollment and retention management.

One staff person should be responsible for the telecounseling program as it relates to enrollment management, and one staff person should be responsible for the telecounseling program on behalf of retention management. Information from phone calls should be evaluated with other research reports and communicated to all appropriate staff members. Finally, it is imperative that the deans of enrollment and retention management act on the information received and change or modify whatever is required. A prompt response to information obtained from telecounseling phone calls can result in effective changes becoming part of a school's overall enrollment and retention management programs and can prevent having to wait until the enrollment period or academic year is over to institute necessary changes.

GETTING STARTED

There are some basics needed for any successful telecounseling program.

- A budget should be established to provide for headsets, telephones, food, office supplies, prizes, and computer equipment.
- Callers should be provided with a comfortable and efficient working area.
- A computer supported tracking system should allow callers to report on their progress in a uniform way.

TRAINING

Someone in the admission or dean of enrollment management's office must assume the responsibility for training the staff that will be used in the telecounseling program. This is especially important if student workers are used since problems of boredom and frustration are most likely to occur with this group. Anticipating and listening to the needs of the telecounselors will help the program to succeed. The following are some basic rules for conducting a telecounseling program:

- Set targets. A certain number of phone calls should be expected each hour, day, and week. If a counselor consistently does not meet the targeted number, the supervisor should meet with the person and discuss the problems and how to solve them.
- Follow a realistic schedule. Observe holidays, exam schedules, pep rallies, and so forth. Allow for breaks. Telecounselors should be able to get up and move about, stretch, get something to eat or drink, or make small talk with a fellow worker. The telecounseling room should be located in a pleasant area.
- Share successes and frustrations. If a particular telephone technique is proving effective, all telecounselors should be informed of it. Counselors who are experiencing frustration should share their concerns with other counselors and solicit their suggestions and support.
- Frequent meetings will allow all of the telecounselors to exchange ideas and information and will allow the director of telecounseling to provide important feedback.
- The program should be evaluated frequently and changes should be made based upon the information received. A computer-assisted tracking and follow-up system should be in place. An annual report of the telecounseling goals and objectives and the results of the program should be shared with all telecounselors.

The phone should not be used only for qualifying the applicant pool. The phone can be used effectively to solicit specific information from other student

cohorts and can and should complement the research component of the enrollment and retention management units.

An effective way to find out why students are leaving your school is simply
to ask those who have left why they did. If phone calls are made in the right
way, most people do not mind receiving them and cooperating with the caller.
This information can and should supplement information from research reports
and data and it is the dean's responsibility to cross-reference this information
and act upon it.

Be prepared to make changes to your enrollment and retention management programs if you receive information from the telecounseling program that suggests
that changes should be made. Otherwise, telecounseling becomes an exercise in
futility.

7

Publications

"Though we cannot affirmatively tell you what we are doing, we can, negatively, tell you what we are not doing—we never once thought of a king."

—First press release from the 1787 Constitutional Convention

I once conducted a workshop at which a few of the participants arrived late and did not know the school I represented or its location. Holding up a sample of our publications, I asked this group to tell me what images the publications conveyed to them. Their responses matched exactly what our research indicated we wished to convey—downtown, urban location, small, student-centered school.

When I first arrived at Suffolk University, I asked to see all of the promotional materials, such as brochures and direct mail pieces. What I was given included over 100 publications. About 80 of the pieces projected a conflicting image and marketing message. The brochures reflected a lack of marketing direction and a focused approach to projecting a consistent image. I remember thinking that if I was confused about what our publications were trying to convey, how could we expect our potential students to get a clear sense of what we had to offer.

Despite extensive research and exhaustive rhetoric about the need for a consistent "look," I know of several colleges and universities whose publications still have a confused marketing message. What may seem obvious and simple to achieve may be more complicated and can often present campus-wide difficulties for the enrollment manager charged with the responsibility of coordinating the school's publications.

No single publication or brochure or direct mail piece will make an applicant enroll at any school. At best, a well-designed publication, one that has a clear marketing message and has been attractively packaged, can result in a prospective applicant requesting more information about your institution, or may prompt the family to visit your campus. Conversely, a poorly designed publication can deter a potential applicant from further investigating your school.

Publications should accurately reflect what a school has to offer. *Reality must match perception.* Slick publications cannot compensate for an inadequate academic program or a high attrition rate.

It is essential to determine the purpose of publications. Do you want potential students to phone and ask for more information? Do you want them to return the reply card? Match the publication to its specific objective. It is important to test the effectiveness and the marketing message of all publications with students *before* they are printed. Publications should be written with students in mind, not faculty, administrators, or trustees.

No one, to the best of my knowledge, has determined with 100% accuracy why some publications are more effective than others. If there were a magic formula, we would all follow it.

MOVING YOUR PUBLICATIONS FROM AN INCONSISTENT LOOK AND CONFUSING MARKETING MESSAGE REQUIRES SEVERAL STEPS

One person, preferably the administrator in charge of enrollment management, should be given the authority to be responsible for all publications specifically targeted to enroll students.

If given a choice between using an outside agency or establishing an internal publications department, I would opt for the latter. Having tried both, I have found that working with university employees was both more efficient and more cost effective than using an external design firm. I have many colleagues who would disagree with this opinion. I have also seen the work of some outside firms who were brought in to "fix" the school's image problems, and after considerable time and money, designed publications that proved to be ineffective.

One of the greatest challenges facing all publications' programs in the future will be how to effectively control and use technology. The interactive, audio-visual "viewbook" is already available in high schools across the country. Families can purchase computer programs to bring campuses into their home for review. The publications of the future will look and feel different, but one thing should always remain the same: a consistent marketing message.

Before too long, electronic viewbooks will be available on the Internet for colleges and universities. Most admission personnel and enrollment managers are just beginning to incorporate their Web site into their overall publications and marketing programs. Home pages allow prospective students to interact in a way not possible with the traditional viewbook. Albion College recently held its first "virtual" open house for prospective students who were able to speak with professors and students from more than 60 "chat rooms." This made the front page of the *Wall Street Journal*.

There should be one central budget line that allocates the money needed to produce publications for the offices of undergraduate and graduate admission, international students' office, the registrar's office, the office of financial aid, continuing education, and corporate outreach. Future budget requests should take into consideration the effectiveness of each publication, the number used, and the ever-changing postal rates.

The analysis of focus groups' information and insights should be taken into consideration before the marketing message is determined and the graphic look designed.

The school's advertising, public relations messages, videos, posters, direct mail, and telecounseling calls should be reviewed for consistency with the school's publications.

The publications' funnel for all market segments, not just the undergraduate market, should be reviewed frequently, and any necessary changes should be made. Resources, including financial ones, should be shifted as needed.

A school-wide image or intergrated marketing committee should be formed to review the messages conveyed to the public from all outreach vehicles. The committee should meet regularly and should include a broad spectrum of the campus community. Students should also be a part of this group. Administrators at Texas-Christian University have been successful in implementing a university wide marketing approach to their publications.

Include the director of public affairs and members of the development, and alumni offices into the meetings of the image committee. The messages conveyed by the publications of these offices, should be consistent with the messages being conveyed to prospective students.

Before you can organize your publications, you must know who your audience is, what you want to say, and how you want to get your message across. One of the best planning forms created and one which I have used in working with department heads and admission counselors was created by Bob Topor of Topor Consultants Group International. This guide asks the hard questions and forces everyone involved in the creative process to think about what they want the brochure, magazine, or direct mail piece to convey. An example of the form follows.

MARKETING PUBLICATIONS PLANNING FORM

Identify your users, current and potential. Who are they? What are their common characteristics in terms of demographics (occupation, education, income, age, sex, race/ethnicity, religion); geodemographics (specific area, population density, climate); and psychographics (lifestyle, personality, self-image, cultural values)?

Users

1. _____
2. _____
3. _____
4. _____
5. _____

Perceived attributes are the basis for all marketing decisions. You can't "sell" undergraduate enrollment to retirees in Florida. If you are considering marketing a "product" (service), make sure you know at least five common attributes as perceived by the target market you are trying to reach.

Service Benefits and Attributes

1. _____
2. _____
3. _____
4. _____
5. _____

Who are your competitors? This may not be an easy question to answer. Competitors aren't the only other institutions offering similar services. If you think those are the only competition you face, you are making the same mistake as the messenger service unworried with new trends in e-mail and faxing.

Competitors

1. _____
2. _____
3. _____
4. _____
5. _____

Do users want and need your offerings? Be objective. Ask current users what they like. Think of the needs your service meets. Are there tangible benefits gained from using your service?

Benefits

1. _____
2. _____
3. _____

4. _____
5. _____

Is your service unique? Make sure you evaluate your school's perceived advantages from the users' point of view and not your own! Colleges and universities are known by their differences, not similarities.

Comparative Differential Advantages

1. _____
2. _____
3. _____
4. _____
5. _____

The following planning form is a shorter version of the form presented above. Consider using one or the other or combine parts of each to create a new form.

1. Has a budget been allocated for this publication? How much is available? Is this amount sufficient for effective distribution?
2. How many copies will be printed? Why? How will the publication be used?
3. Describe the program/service.
4. Define the target audiences. To whom is this publication directed? Define audiences and constituencies in hierarchical order.
5. What is this publication supposed to accomplish? Define objectives in order of priority.
6. Describe three key ideas this publication should communicate. What are the benefits to the user?
7. How will this publication be distributed? Who will distribute it?
8. Describe competitors. How do their services compete with yours?
9. How will the publication's results be measured? How will the results be reported? To whom?

VIEWBOOKS

Remember when the viewbook was considered the "revolutionary" replacement for the catalog? If you were responsible for enrollment in the early 1980s, you will remember that creating a slick four-color publication was considered by many to be too "commercial" and smacked of "hucksterism." Many faculty and admission "gatekeepers" derided its use and effectiveness. I know I will upset more than one college administrator with this next opinion. I believe that the viewbook is already obsolete and will soon be replaced by technology.

Recently my daughter completed the college application process. Like many families throughout the country, we received nearly 200 "propaganda" pieces, most unsolicited. I reviewed all of the search and direct mail pieces with her, interested in getting her reaction to each school's initial marketing piece. Typically, she gave about three minutes of her attention to the publications she received. The materials she put aside were those from each of the schools that she had some prior interest in further investigating. There were about five, out of 200 schools, whose marketing message was so strong that she thought *perhaps* she should contact the school for more information! The money spent on these 200 publications exceeded my entire publications' budget for the year and could finance more than a few college tuitions.

So why do we all continue to use this method of distributing our information? Are our marketing messages, conveyed in viewbooks, so strong that they are able to change an eighteen-year-old's opinion about our schools? I doubt it. I believe that viewbook distribution is an example of following the crowd. To me, it is the result of insecurity based on the false belief that if we don't buy thousands of names and mail them our search piece and viewbook, we will lose market share. In my opinion, it reflects a lack of current and valid research on who are our strongest prospects. This type of mass mailing fails to target specific markets and wastes a great deal of time and money.

Have you ever heard of a high school senior who thought receiving 200 pieces of unsolicited "propaganda" mail was great? After the first blush, the novelty of receiving so much mail fades and most of our beautifully designed publications are never read and wind up in the wastebasket.

Most viewbooks don't convey a clear sense of what they want to accomplish. Consequently, potential students don't know what to do with the materials when they arrive (unsolicited) at their home. Few viewbooks have a clear "call to action." Many viewbooks look the same. You know the ones I mean. The sun is shinning and all the students are smiling. Each publication should have a justification for its existence, should focus on what makes the school unique from other schools, and should attempt to look and be different in some way. Few do.

So many of the viewbooks sent to families across the country are mismatched. Why, for example, would a small, Methodist school in the Midwest send literature to an eastern, private, Catholic girls' school applicant? (This actually happened to my daughter.) Oftentimes, money is wasted on sending the information to the wrong or inappropriate audience and stressing quantity over quality.

With many schools, once the viewbook is mailed there is little or no follow-up. Of the 200 schools that sent literature to my daughter, fewer than 20 made further contact with her. What happened to the others? Why did they send the initial piece? What was the purpose of the publication? Did they want her to request further information, or request an application? Their marketing message was not clear. There was no follow-up piece or telecounseling phone call. No net gain to anyone except the printers and post office.

Most of the viewbooks come at the same time. From spring of the junior year to the following fall, our mailbox groaned with the weight of college publications. Once again the timing of viewbook distribution makes it difficult to differentiate one school from another. Few high school juniors and seniors will spend the time to analyze each school's materials. Either the publication will be so strong as to be pulled out of the pack (George Washington's pieces are an excellent example of this) or it won't. For most schools, the latter prediction is often more accurate than the former.

AN ALTERNATIVE TO THE VIEWBOOK

So what is the alternative to the viewbook? One alternative is to create a more "user friendly" publication that can accomplish for your marketing program what the viewbook once did. I know of one school which used its viewbook funding to create two magazines. While other schools have one "hit" with their viewbook, this school gets two. They are able to send their second magazine after most other schools have expended their publications' budget on one viewbook. It costs less to produce the two magazines than it did to create one viewbook. Still not convinced? The research team conducted focus groups of high school students and asked them to compare some of the old viewbooks with the new magazines. All preferred the magazines over the viewbook. One of the results of introducing the magazine concept to replace the viewbook was increased attendance at information sessions. Remember the mailings were targeted and the applicant pool was qualified in a variety of ways. Magazines were sent only to propsective applicants interested in receiving them.

Another reason for reconsidering the use of your school's viewbook is the rapid and ongoing changes in communications brought about by tremendous technological advances. Within a short period of time, all schools will have home pages on the Internet. Future applicants will have at their fingertips instant access to information about any school. Enrollment managers should be involved in establishing the marketing message and image that can be effectively projected on the "net." A school-wide image committee should begin now to grapple with the long-term effects of technology on future publications.

There are several companies that are currently creating what I call a "virtual viewbook," a CD-ROM program that presents to prospective applicants a visual and audio image of a school. This is not some futuristic fantasy. Currently, seniors in about 300 selected high schools across the country have an opportunity to learn about Suffolk University by flipping a switch. Communicating with our future student body technologically is here to stay. It's another reason to rethink the viewbook and its effectiveness in your marketing strategy.

UNDERGRADUATE ADMISSION FUNNEL

The timing and nature of the information sent to prospective applicants and their families will depend, in large measure, on the market position of the school and the undergraduate admission office's marketing plan for the upcoming year. It has always been my opinion that a successful funnel will consistently move a prospect from the initial point of contact to filing an application and if applicable, accepting an offer of admission and enrolling. Frequent follow-up is necessary. However, you must have something to tell the prospect, and the perception of what you are "selling" must match reality. At each stage of the funnel, it should be apparent what the desired outcome is. Do you want to encourage the prospect to seek further information about the school, to obtain an early estimate of financial aid, to visit the school, to schedule an interview, or to apply? The funnel should support and be consistent with other marketing messages and contacts, including videos, advertising, direct mail letters and telecounseling calls.

I was amazed at the number of colleges and universities contacting my daughter during the early stage of the application process. However, few schools attempted to move her to the next phase of it. She received no telecounseling phone call from any of the colleges or universities that had sent her their initial recruitment piece. With the exception of about twenty schools, out of nearly 200, she received no follow-up material. She applied to none of the schools as a result of their initial publications. I have to wonder why so much paper (I hope it was recycled) was sent to our house in the first place. Unless you can send out consistent and frequent publications, don't waste money on sending an initial piece. Decide on the prospects you want to target and then pursue them with well-timed, focused, and meaningful contacts.

The following undergraduate admission "funnel" is one that I have used over the years and have modified to suit the needs of the prospect pool and the market position of the school.

1. Search piece—April of junior year
2. College night or fair brochure—June of junior year
3. Personalized letter sent from the admission office—Summer
4. Magazine #1 with application—Summer
5. Informational packet sent to parents—Summer
6. Visit brochure—Summer
7. Faculty letter—Summer
8. Second personalized letter from the admission office—Summer
9. Telecounseling call by current student—Fall through Summer
10. Magazine #2—October
11. Early financial aid application invitation—October
12. Undergraduate admission and financial aid newsletter—November
13. Invitation to open house—November
14. Estimate of financial aid mailed to family—January

15. Phone call to families receiving early financial estimates—January
16. Career brochure—February
17. Departmental newsletters mailed to prospective majors—February
18. Admission decision letter mailed—March
19. Financial aid award letter mailed—March
20. Invitation to reception for accepted applicants—March
21. Faculty phone call to accepted candidates—Mary
22. Letter to parents from the president—March
23. Retention packet mailed—April
24. Outcomes packet mailed—April
25. Admission phone-a-thon to accepted applicants—April
26. Registration packet and housing information mailed—May
27. Orientation information mailed—May
28. Summer "meltdown" telecounseling phone calls—June, July, August
29. Letter to parents of enrolled students from the dean—September
30. Letter to enrolled students and parents from alumni—October

The effectiveness or ineffectiveness of this funnel should be assessed by your student-clients. During orientation the director of enrollment research should survey all of the enrolled students to evaluate the information he or she received during the application process. After that, small focus groups should further analyze what was sent and when it was sent. The same process should take place with high school students. Ask these potential customers to tell you if they are receiving the intended marketing message. Consistently, the majority of applicants, high school students, and enrolled students polled have rated the quality, quantity, and message of our funnel as good or excellent. About 77% of the enrolled students indicated that the amount of direct mail they received from Suffolk was just about right; 60% rated the quality of the information received as good; and 27% rated the publications as excellent.

Fifteen Publications Suggestions

1. Publications should reflect the marketing message as defined by your constituency through valid and current research.
2. Develop a look and style that fits the image you wish to convey.
3. Be consistent in the logo, design, and color in each of your publications. All your publications should look as if they belong to the same "family."
4. Use quality paper stock, recycled if possible. Since paper costs have increased substantially in the past few years, you will want to shop around for the best prices.
5. Use off-white or cream color as a background color instead of stark white. It's much easier on the eyes.
6. Use a good writer with a proven track record and someone with whom you can work in a creative and enjoyable way.

7. Create publications for your prospective customers, not for the president, faculty, or even yourself.
8. Try to design a different size or shape for your major publication; something that is both visually attractive and unique.
9. Create a different design with the outside of the envelope. It could be a reason why the high school junior or senior opens your direct mail piece and reads your marketing message.
10. Remember to stress *benefits* rather than *features.*
11. Observe what your competition is doing and come up with something better.
12. Try to produce publications which can be used more than once. You don't want to be in the position of having to change your look every year.
13. Both the editorial messages and graphic designs should be consistent.
14. Test each of your publications with your prospective clients *before* they are produced.
15. Photographs should tell a story, not just show a pretty face or attractive building. Make your photographs illustrate something special about your school, something that is different from your competitors.

If given a choice, I would always recommend having an internal publications department. You can't expect an outside firm or group of people to understand your college or university the way internal personnel can. The trick is to hire the right people to do the job. You can expect this type of arrangement to be cost effective. The same publication team that designs publications for you can also design publications for the president, the development office and the alumni director. All of the university's publications should have a similar look and should convey the same message to the various outside constituencies. If you want to see a good example of this, try to get your hands on some of Mike Feinstein's publications for Georgetown's Bicentennial celebrations. In my opinion, these are the best in the business.

If organized properly, publications can make a significant contribution to a school's overall enrollment management program. For me it's one of the most creative and enjoyable aspects of my job. Working with creative designers and writers and seeing the marketing pieces move from the talking stage to real life is very exciting.

It is important to remember that publications alone will not fill classrooms. The publication and direct mail programs of our schools can only reflect what it is the school is and what it can offer to prospective applicants.

8

Advertising

"80 percent of your business comes from 20 percent of your customers."

—Swim with the Sharks Without Being Eaten Alive

I will make the assumption that most people reading this book are totally or partially responsible for their school's advertising program, or are working toward having that responsibility. I will further assume that you have or are questioning whether you are getting the most from your advertising dollars. If so, I recommend the following.

Twenty Advertising Observations and Suggestions

1. Advertising cannot fill empty classrooms or turn an unpopular major into a popular one. Students don't enroll in colleges and universities because of great ads.
2. Advertising can create awareness, help establish an image, or prompt a prospective student to phone for a brochure or application.
3. This may sound like a basic but it is often overlooked: be certain everyone involved in the advertising process has agreed in principle on the purpose and objective of the advertising program.
4. One campus administrator should coordinate and have the overall responsibility for a school's advertising program. Having many people or individ-

ual departments prepare specific program ads will result in an inconsistent marketing message.

5. A school's advertising program should be part of its overall marketing plan and should be consistent with the external message communicated by the school's publications and public relations campaign. All of these marketing vehicles should be consistent with reality. They should reflect what a school really has to offer.

6. An advertising program should be planned for an entire year, and contingency funds should be set aside to develop ads for new academic programs.

7. Before budget requests are made, determine what it is you wish to accomplish with your advertising program. Are you interested primarily in creating awareness of your school or a new program? Do you want to expand a current market or develop a new one? Having a clear set of advertising goals and objectives will facilitate the planning process.

8. Base your advertising program on solid research and focus group analysis. Know why people respond to your ads, which ads they are responding to, and what the yields are for each of your ads. Use coupons to track your advertising responses.

9. Keep a list of everyone who responds to your ads. Monitor this group to etermine whether they enroll and if not, why. Send information on a regular basis to the people on this list about new programs and courses. If possible, communicate with them by phone. Find out from your potential customers what courses they would like to take, when they would like to take them, and why.

10. The frequency and consistency of ads are essential to effective advertising. Don't dilute the effectiveness of your campaign by allocating insufficient funds in several different arenas. If you don't have enough money to do well all of the advertising you want, select the most important vehicles and then pay for a frequent and consistent message to be communicated. Depending upon the size of the school, its image or awareness problems, the number of programs it plans to advertise, and the location of the school, an advertising program can cost from $1,000,000 to $3,000,000 per year. That may sound like a great deal of money. I know several schools that allocate more than this amount to their advertising campaigns. It all depends on needs, resources, and results. Are the ads generating "leads"? Are the "leads" converting into applications? Enrollments? Good research is necessary to evaluate any advertising program.

11. Remember to direct your ads to your audience: students. Don't create ads to please faculty, administrators, or even yourself. Those groups are not the target audience.

12. Attractive graphics, catchy headlines, and repetition of a clear message are the keys to a good advertising program.

13. If you hire an outside advertising firm, be certain you thoroughly investigate their track record from previous clients.

14. If you don't use an outside firm, you will need to divide the advertising responsibilities along creative and administrative lines. Appoint an account representative, someone who can place the ads and deal with the sales representatives. Another staff person will be needed to design the ads and generate the copy.

15. Investigate the costs for advertising on television, including cable, on radio, trains, buses, and billboards.

16. Advertising in high school and transfer school newspapers is an effective and inexpensive way to reach those two potential markets.

17. Advertising in local newspapers and dailies will get the attention of adult students who may be interested in continuing their education. This is also a good vehicle to communicate with graduate students and corporate clients.

18. Compare your school's ads with those of your competitors. But don't copy another school's ads. Maintain your individuality and marketing message. Remember you can only "sell" what you have to offer.

19. Ideally, if all of your ads were placed next to each other, the image they are projecting should be a clear and consistent one. Advertising should complement the overall marketing plan and the publications and public relations campaigns.

20. Evaluate your current year's program before planning for next year's campaign. Make any necessary changes and listen to what your customers tell you.

Every semester the directors of public relations, advertising, and publications should meet with the dean of enrollment management. This image or intergated marketing committee should meet for the purpose of coordinating each of the activities as they relate to the overall enrollment management plan and to be certain each department is "on the same page" in projecting the school's image. It is imperative that in some way and to a great extent, a school's advertising, publications, and public relations announcements all match. The message should be a clear and consistent one and should complement one another. Each year's campaign should build upon the previous year and should strengthen the marketing message.

9

The Role of Faculty in Enrollment and Retention Management

"One cannot discover what makes a school bad, better or best by reading the catalogue or studying the curriculum. What distinguishes one school from another are often subtle, perhaps invisible qualities that reflect the basic character of the faculty. Only we ourselves know whether we have been involved in a quality education effort. If the answer is yes, it is not a reflection or result of any pedagogical innovation or education gimmickry. Quality resulted because we cared about our students, placed their interests before our own, and gave them the best we had to offer."

—Unattributed
Journal of Dental Education

Few college administrators and faculty members would dispute that financial issues play a significant role in higher education. Decreased enrollments, high attrition rates, and significant decreases in federal and state funding all have contributed to many colleges and universities struggling to stay in the black each year. Several schools have closed their doors in the last twenty years and many others have merged or consolidated their programs with other institutions.

Every campus constituency competes for the dollars that are available to spend. Do you add another admission counselor or an additional English teacher? Do you lower academic standards to retain more students or do you increase remediation courses? Tension for resources is a reality on most college campuses.

A university is a community of faculty teaching a body of students. There can be no enrollment and retention management without faculty input and cooperation. Remember, the admission office is the sales office. Counselors can only market to potential students what they have to "sell." And what they have to sell are the academic programs and courses the institution offers and the faculty who teach them. Any attempt to increase enrollments by adding new courses or programs to the curriculum must be a cooperative effort between faculty and administrators.

I know of one university with an energetic and creative enrollment manager who committed a fatal mistake: failing to ask for faculty assistance and unwilling to listen to faculty concerns about a suggested new program. Without faculty support, and with senior management remaining unconvinced of the need for the new program, the initiative died before it had a chance to succeed. If you are a higher education administrator and you are reading this section of the book, you are silently saying to yourself that if you wait for faculty consensus, nothing will ever happen. Faculty march to a different drummer. They want to think and reflect, then meet in large committees to discuss the best way to proceed. I have made several mistakes trying to get new programs through the system without taking into account the people who will be most affected by programmatic changes: the faculty. A balance between the urgency perceived by the enrollment manager and the faculty's need to reflect can and should be met. Without faculty support for new ideas and programs and without faculty willingness to assist in the recruitment and retention programs, the best enrollment and retention managers will undoubtedly fail.

Since a significant component of a retention management program's success depends upon faculty-student advising, it is essential to obtain faculty input and cooperation. It should be made clear to faculty that retention management is not about lowering standards and keeping students in school at any cost. What should be stressed is that any successful retention management program rests primarily with the faculty. It is the faculty who most often interact with students and it is the faculty who can most influence a student's decision to stay in school or withdraw.

Ways in Which Enrollment and Retention Management Programs Can Assist Faculty

- The dean of enrollment management should meet every semester with the faculty in each department. Enrollment challenges, new initiatives and a discussion of faculty's observations should form the basis of these meetings. This exchange also allows faculty to voice their concerns to the dean on the quality of the students enrolled, class sizes, and course scheduling.

- If the dean of enrollment management has a centralized publications department and budget, a recruitment brochure for each department should be written and printed.
- If the dean of enrollment management has a centralized advertising budget, ads can be prepared for specific majors and programs.
- Throughout the recruitment cycle, the undergraduate and graduate admission offices should send to each departmental chairperson a list of prospective students in their major. Faculty can contact applicants and play a significant role in the admission process while at the same time helping to increase the number of students in their major.
- The dean of enrollment management should convene an undergraduate and graduate admission council, which would meet regularly and solicit faculty input and suggestions. These councils also provide an opportunity for the dean to distribute information on current enrollment trends and projections as well as present information on enrollment threats and challenges. I used to meet each semester with faculty from each department at Suffolk University to explain the results of our marketing and admission programs and to discuss the latest retention efforts. I also came to these meetings prepared to listen to faculty complaints and suggestions. These exchanges became the cornerstone of building a healthy and mutual respect for what each of us was trying to accomplish for the University. I believe that many of the new initiatives later introduced met with little or no resistance because both sides understood why the programs were being offered and how everyone would benefit.
- The dean of retention management should provide each academic unit with its semester attrition and retention rates.
- The dean of retention management can provide information to each academic unit on the students in their major who stopped out, dropped out, or who officially withdrew.
- The retention management committee should include selected faculty who can bring the faculty's perspective on retention issues to the attention of the committee.
- Faculty advising should be recognized and rewarded.
- Each semester every faculty member should receive the results of the school's enrollment and retention management programs. A campus-wide newsletter highlighting the programs' successes and failures should be distributed by the deans of enrollment and retention management.

There are many other ways in which faculty can be included in a school's enrollment and retention management programs. The school's culture, the severity of the school's enrollment and retention problems, and the current state of finances will, to a large extent, determine how faculty interact in enrollment and retention management. One thing is certain: enrolling students and retaining them cannot succeed without faculty assistance and cooperation.

10

Financial Aid

"Can anyone remember when the times were not hard and money not scarce?"

—Ralph Waldo Emerson

I think we would all agree that the college students of tomorrow will be different in many ways from today's students. As with many other aspects of higher education administration, the ways families pay for college and a school's financial aid and debt management programs will need to change to meet tomorrow's financial realities.

Consider the Following

- According to the College Board, tuition at private colleges and universities has increased by 90% since 1980 and by 100% at public institutions.
- The National Association of Independent Colleges and Universities, reports that federal and state funding decreased approximately 24% during the 1980s.
- In the 1980s, a Pell Grant covered 38% of the average cost of a private, four year university. Today, it covers 14%. For public schools, Pell grants covered 82% of costs in 1980. Today, those grants can cover as little as 34%.

- Future federal student aid funding is likely to be in the form of loans, not grants. Currently, loans represent 56% of all available aid. Grants represent 44% of the total federal, state, and institutional aid.
- Funding for higher education in some states will decrease.
- Institutional funding, at both private and state schools, is likely to continue to increase. Currently, college and university grant funding exceeds $3 billion per year.
- Students and their parents are likely to assume a greater responsibility for meeting educational costs.
- Students may have to work more hours to meet a portion of their educational expenses.
- Career planning will continue to be an integral part of a student's college choice.
- "Bidding wars" for students, already in evidence, are likely to increase.
- Some colleges will be forced to abandon their need-blind admission policies.
- There is evidence to support the contention that students are taking longer to complete their undergraduate education. In the future more students may drop from full-time to part-time status in an attempt to reduce costs and borrowing.
- High school students, especially minority students, may decide not to enroll in college, fearing high tuition and unmanageable student debt.
- Some college graduates may postpone graduate school enrollment because of high undergraduate debt.
- A new type of "regionalism" may occur with a school's geographic location playing a major role in enrollment choice. To save costs, students will enroll closer to home.
- A stratification of enrollment, along economic lines, may occur with the children of the rich enrolling in the most expensive and prestigious schools.
- Colleges and universities will be forced to look at their financial aid policies and programs and their impact on attrition rates.

In a 1995 report, *Money* magazine polled families of college age children and asked about the importance of finances in their enrollment selection. Of the families polled, 67% indicated that financial considerations influenced their choice of college. This represents an increase from 61% the previous year. This data makes it clear that institutional financial aid offers are important to freshmen in deciding which college to attend.

Forecasts are never made with absolute certainty. However, one trend cannot be disputed: the funding of higher education will change in the future. Students and their families will assume a greater responsibility for meeting educational costs. The role of the federal government in student financing may continue to decrease, and it remains to be determined what role state governments will assume. Students will take longer to complete their degrees. More students will work longer hours to help meet their expenses. More students will borrow more money to finance their education. Schools will continue to "discount" their published tuition rates. Change. Change. Change.

THE ROLE OF FINANCIAL AID IN ENROLLMENT MANAGEMENT

In an earlier section of this book I indicated that it is my strong belief that there can be no effective enrollment management program without the synergistic interaction between the recruitment and admission programs and a school's financial aid program. I further believe that all schools should consider the role that their financial aid policies play in their retention and attrition rates.

Each year it becomes more and more apparent that financial considerations are becoming the *primary* reason for enrollment or for non-enrollment at many schools. Ability to pay has little to do with willingness to pay. It should come as no surprise that increasingly, the family income profile at many public institutions is fast approaching that of private schools. For many families, there is no perceived cost benefit in attending a high priced, private institution. This trend is likely to continue in the future.

The effective administration of a school's financial aid program depends upon a packaging philosophy that is consistent with the mission of the school and the goals of its admission and retention programs. One of the early goals of financial aid was to eliminate the financial barrier to higher education. However, as the competition for students increased, the role of financial aid changed. The marketing position of a college or university began to influence, and in some cases dictate, the school's financial aid program. In recruiting students, competitive financial aid packages became an important part in enhancing a school's market position. Financial aid administrators, once considered merely federal and state aid processors, became major players in developing and implementing their school's marketing, admission, enrollment, and retention programs.

As federal and state financial aid subsidies decreased, it became increasingly necessary for schools to increase the amount of institutional funds they distributed to prospective and enrolled students. In many cases, institutional monies were used to attract the more academically qualified applicants and less to make college affordable to economically disadvantaged students. While access is the opportunity to enroll in an institution of higher education, choice is the opportunity to choose among schools which meet a student's academic and career needs, academic capability, *and* family income.

In a "Postsecondary Education Opportunity" newsletter, author Tom Mortenson conducted a study on the growing importance of financial considerations in college choice from 1980 to 1994 and reports the following.

- Between 1989 and 1994, the greatest growth in the importance of a financial aid offer in the college choice decision was for freshmen from families with parental incomes above $80,000.

- Between 1980 and 1994, the proportion of college freshmen reporting that the offer of student financial assistance was very important to their college choice decision increased from 16% to nearly 30%. Similarly, the proportion of freshmen reporting that low tuition was very important in their college choice decision increased from 17% to 29%.

- The importance of a financial aid offer in the college choice decision is becoming more and more important to freshmen entering both private and public colleges and universities.

There is some evidence to suggest that some middle income applicants are shifting their enrollments from private schools to public institutions in order to capture the institutional subsidy not based on financial need that they no longer qualify for through federal and state-mandated needs tests. Private colleges and universities no longer compete with each other on the basis of stated price. They compete primarily on the basis of general academic reputation, enhanced services and programs, and discounted tuition price. The non-grant components of financial aid, loans and employment, appear to have little influence on where a student enrolls. Two factors that do appear to have some influence on college choice is when the student is notified of financial aid and the student's perception that the offer of financial assistance will continue after the first year.

Since it is critical that the marketing, admission, and retention programs be synergistic with a school's financial aid program, enrollment managers should assess the integration of the offices and programs by asking the following questions:

1. The admission and financial aid programs are:
   —totally integrated
   —somewhat integrate
   —not integrated at all
2. Financial aid policies are determined by:
   —admission director
   —financial aid director
   —budget officer
   —senior administrator
   —combination of administrators
3. What is the packaging philosophy of your school? Can it respond to the school's changing student population? How has your school's financial aid program affected the school's attrition and retention rates? What does the research indicate?
4. What does it cost to educate one student at your institution? What amount of money is available in endowment funds for institutional financial aid?
5. Is your school's packaging philosophy consistent with the mission of the school and with the goals of the recruitment and admission programs?

6. What percentage of the incoming class will receive financial aid? What percentage of transfer students and returning students receive financial assistance? How has this changed over the years?

7. Are there different packaging philosophies for different student-cohorts? If yes, what has been the yields in each category? How is financial aid utilized in the recruiting program? Can the financial aid program be changed to respond to the school's changing demographic or market position needs?

8. Do you offer different financial aid packages to the following groups:
   —academically talented students
   —students with special talents
   —students in specific or preferred majors
   —female students
   —minority students
   —international students
   —adult learners
   —part-time students
   —middle income students

9. Do you know which financial aid policies are most and least effective with regard to meeting enrollment targets? What does the research indicate?

10. What percentage of the school's budget is allocated to financial aid? How has that allocation changed over the last five years? Is it sufficient to compete in the marketplace? What does the research indicate?

11. Do you provide applicants with an early estimate of their financial aid awards? If yes, what is the yield for prospects participating in the service?

12. When are accepted applicants informed of their financial aid awards? Has that timing changed over the past five years? If yes, what has been the result on enrollment yields?

13. Is financial aid awarded on a first come, first served basis or are monies allocated for specific cohorts of students regardless of the time of application?

14. What percentage of a family's income would be needed to fund one year at your school?

15. Is it possible to "unbundle" costs so that specific services could be charged separately?

16. Are your financial aid filing procedures complex and/or punitive, or is the process informative, easy, and user friendly?

17. Does the school provide a family with a financial planning program, including options for payment?

18. What was the average indebtedness of last year's graduating class? Is debt management counseling made available?

19. What is the relationship between the admission and financial aid offices? Are there synergistic processes in place for both functions?

20. If one aspect of the school's financial aid program could be changed, what should (or could) it be?

Information that Should Be Shared with Your School's Financial Aid Personnel

1. The school's enrollment targets from its primary, secondary and tertiary markets
2. The school's *net revenue* needs
3. The school's enrollment challenges and problems
4. Competitor schools' financial aid policies
5. Changes in competitor schools
6. Profile of the incoming freshmen and transfer classes and the financial aid awarded to these two cohorts
7. Profile of the incoming and transfer students who did not enroll and the financial aid awarded to those two cohorts
8. Profile of the incoming graduate school students and the financial aid awarded to those who enrolled and those who did not
9. Analysis of all students who withdrew and their financial aid awards
10. Analysis of what the school's financial aid dollars "bought." Did the admission and financial aid programs complement each other to achieve the desired enrollment and retention goals?

Information that Should Be Shared with Your School's Admission Counselors

1. Current changes in federal and state financial aid policies that may affect the school's financial aid program
2. The impact of the early estimator (if you use one) on enrollment yields
3. The packaging philosophy for each student-cohort and the relationship between the amount of financial aid awarded and enrollment yields
4. The packaging philosophy for continuing students and the impact on the school's retention and attrition rates
5. How a financial aid package is determined, including the scholarship, grant, loan, and employment components of the package
6. All of the merit scholarships available to incoming and transfer students and the criteria for receiving the award
7. The financial aid application process, including the forms used, the deadlines for submitting applications, the notification and the appeal processes
8. How to handle questions about the classification of dependent and independent student status, the calculation of need, reporting outside awards, the impact of savings on the financial aid award, how to decline a portion of the financial aid award, and how to state extenuating circumstances
9. The payment options available to all families
10. How financial need is determined and the average amount of unmet need

11. The major loan programs and the general conditions for each of the programs as well as the repayment terms
12. The average loan indebtedness of students after the first, second, and third years and the average indebtedness of graduating seniors
13. The role of employment in the financial aid package and how employment funds are calculated in the school's billing procedures
14. The school's appeal process and the options for students who want to enroll but cannot afford to do so
15. The school's discounting policies

An important part of integrating a school's admission and financial aid programs is publishing annual statistics, which should be shared with everyone in the divisions of enrollment and retention management as well as other senior staff members. If the admission, financial aid and retention programs are truly complementing one another, it will be apparent from these semester and annual statistics that the financial aid policies contributed to meeting the school's enrollment and retention goals.

FINANCIAL AID REPORTS

In order to determine whether your school's financial aid policies and programs are effective and are assisting in meeting the enrollment and retention goals, semester and annual reports should be produced, including the following.

1. The number of freshmen, transfers, and graduate students who were admitted, awarded financial aid and enrolled
2. The number of freshmen, transfers, and graduate students who were admitted but did not enroll and the financial aid awarded to these cohorts
3. The type and average amount of financial aid awarded to all enrolled students
4. The type and average amount of financial aid awarded to all students who declined admission
5. The average amount of institutional aid awarded to admitted and enrolled applicants and admitted but non-enrolled applicants
6. The average amount of non-institutional aid awarded to both groups of applicants
7. The relationship between tuition costs and average institutional aid awards
8. The average institutional award as a percentage of tuition
9. The average discounted tuition of enrolled students
10. Comparison of average discounted tuition rates of competitor schools
11. The profile of students who received more financial assistance from other institutions, including the type and amount of aid received
12. The enrollment rates for new students offered only merit-based aid
13. The enrollment rates for new students offered only need-based aid
14. The recruitment areas of new, full-paying students

15. The parental income of full-paying students
16. How full-paying students meet their educational expenses
17. The retention rates of full-paying students
18. The retention rates for all returning students receiving financial aid
19. The retention rates for all returning students receiving only loans and employment
20. The retention rates for students receiving no financial assistance
21. The type and average financial aid award of all students who withdraw
22. The unmet need of students
23. The income levels of applicants and students applying for financial aid
24. The academic profile of all applicants and students who do not apply for financial aid
25. The academic profile of all applicants and enrolled students who are awarded aid and those who are not
26. A comparison of loan and grant ratios
27. The role of student debt in enrollment and retention
28. The role of student employment in enrollment and retention
29. The average number of hours worked each week
30. How financial aid is helping to meet the objectives of a school's enrollment management and retention programs

NET TUITION

Frequently, college presidents and admission officers will indicate that applications for the year have substantially increased, a sure indication that the admission, financial aid, and enrollment management program is doing its job. What is seldom mentioned is whether deposits have increased, if the "summer melt" has decreased, and if the revenue, after subtracting institutional financial aid, is more or less than that of the previous year. What admission officers will rarely indicate is whether the school met its net tuition revenue needs.

Net tuition, or the money remaining after institutional funds are distributed, has not been, until recently, the "job" of either the admission or financial aid programs. The reason for this is because admission and financial aid personnel rarely knew what the school's net tuition revenue needs were.

Meeting a school's net tuition revenue needs demands a synergistic integration of the recruitment, financial aid, and retention programs. None of the programs can be successful if the budget people have not communicated to the admission and financial aid staffs how much net revenue the school needs in order to balance the budget. Admission counselors, in addition to financial aid personnel, budget officials, and the deans of enrollment and retention management, should agree on what this number should be and how it can be realistically achieved.

One possible outcome of this kind of communication is likely to be the agreement to recruit a certain percentage of students who can afford to pay full tuition without any institutional subsidy. Many colleges and universities have aggressively recruited international students for this reason. This can be effective up to a point. No one would disagree that international students bring a vitality and diversity that are welcome additions to any college campus. However, if a college or university continues to enroll larger and larger classes of international students, it will loose its national and local identity and constituency as well as the reason for its founding. Also, as technology changes the way we deliver educational programs in the future, fewer international students may travel to American campuses. They may stay at home and take courses through distance learning programs at much cheaper costs.

Information Necessary to Determine the Discount Which Will Allow Your School to Reach Its Net Tuition Needs

1. The number of students, new and returning, who pay full tuition
2. The number of students, new and returning, who are likely to receive federal and state aid
3. The number of students, new and returning, who do not apply for aid
4. The number of new students who enrolled in other schools because your financial aid package was not competitive
5. The number of students who leave each semester and year for financial reasons
6. The number of full- and part-time students
7. Internal factors affecting the recruitment, admission, financial aid, and retention programs
8. External factors affecting the recruitment, admission, financial aid, and retention programs
9. Changes in federal and state financial funding policies
10. Changes in endowment funds and the amount allocated for institutional aid
11. Changes in the school's market position
12. Analysis of the students who enrolled and the financial aid awarded and the students who declined enrollment and the financial aid awarded
13. Calculation of the "bottom line" as determined by your school's finance personnel
14. Agreement between the admission, financial aid, and budget staffs on the maximum tuition discounted rate that would allow the school to reach its net tuition revenue needs
15. Careful analysis of a school's financial aid program, market position, and budgetary needs should be analyzed along with the recruitment, enrollment and retention realities of the school; they should all complement one another

EARLY FINANCIAL AID ESTIMATOR

If recent trends are any indication, and I believe they are, finances will continue to play a major role in the college selection process. One way to assist
families in determining whether they can afford to attend your school is to offer
an estimate of what the family is likely to receive in federal, state, and institutional funds. I am not referring to filling out a complicated form which requires
everything short of a pint of blood to complete. What I am suggesting is that
schools develop a simple institutional form to evaluate a family's ability to pay
for college. To be effective, this has to be done during the beginning of the
application cycle. Admission counselors should be armed with early estimator
forms and should distribute them during high school visits and fairs. The estimator forms should also be a part of the early admission "funnel" pieces. The
telecounseling program should remind students and parents of the value of the
early estimator. The research arm of the school's enrollment management program should track which students who enrolled used the early estimator form.
The financial aid office staff should monitor how close the early estimator award
was to the actual award and make any necessary modifications. The entire process should be reviewed by the dean of enrollment management and the financial
aid staff to determine how the early estimator assisted in meeting the goals of
the marketing and admission programs.

Timing is critical in making financial aid awards. Research indicates that
some families will accept the first offer of aid they receive rather than wait for
later offers. The early estimator is an excellent way to qualify the part of your
applicant pool that wants and needs the security of an early estimate of their
financial aid award. Like everything else in the college selection and enrollment
process, there are no guarantees. However, this service can help a recruitment
program, especially if your competitors are not offering it.

When this process is done right, it can be very supportive in helping a school
reach its targeted enrollment needs. The first time we used an early estimator at
Suffolk, 36% of the enrolling class used the service and 75% of all families who
filled out the form found it useful. Instead of scaring people away from applying to a school, an early estimator can provide families with financial information which may indicate that they can afford a school. If costs are too high and
the early estimator indicates that, it is better and more equitable to everyone
involved if this is known in December, rather than in May. It will save you a
lot of time and money and helps to qualify your prospect or applicant pool. It
can save a family the stress of finding out after acceptance that they cannot afford your tuition.

On the other hand when the process is not done well or the offices of admission and financial aid are in conflict over using the form, or the applicants are
not properly tracked, it is a fruitless exercise and a wasted opportunity.

Before beginning the early estimator process, it will be necessary to have not
only the cooperation of the admission and financial aid offices but also some
assistance from the management information (computer) personnel at your

school. You can use an outside firm and pay a great deal of money to develop a computer program to estimate financial or you can use your school's institutional resources and develop your own calculation.

Take your computer folks out to lunch and ask them how you can develop with them a model for estimating a family's financial need. You will need to include the following information

1. General information on the prospective student, including name, address, social security number, address, state of legal residence, high school, class rank, SAT or ACT scores, GPA, age, marital status, citizen or permanent resident status, and year of enrollment
2. Student financial information, including income, cash, savings and checking amounts, investment income, and debt
3. Parental information, including the number of members in the family and the number enrolled in college, the marital status of the parents, actual income for the previous year, estimated income for the current year, adjusted gross income (Line 30 of 1040 or Line 3 of 1040 EZ), taxes paid, income of father and mother, non-taxable income (including social security benefits, aid to dependent children, child support and other non-taxable income), IRA or Keogh payments, medical expenses not covered by insurance, tuition for other children in school, amount of cash, savings and money in checking accounts, home value (this is up to each school to determine if they want to use this in the calculation; home value was removed from the federal calculation), investments and real estate holdings, and current value of business or farm properties

The early estimator forms should be distributed by September 1 of the senior year of high school, and the deadline for submission of the form should be no later than December 15. It is essential that families be informed as soon as possible (two weeks would be ideal). Information on each prospective student completing the early estimator form should be communicated to the admission counselors, who should follow up with a phone call to each family receiving an estimated amount of aid. The enrollment researcher should track applicants using the form with enrolled students and should compare the estimate with the actual award. The dean of enrollment management should review this information with the directors of admission and financial aid and, based on the research information, make adjustments to the program.

It may sound redundant, but the admission and financial aid personnel must work closely together for the service to be effective. Find out if any of your competitors are using an early estimator. The service is most effective if you are the only school offering it. Attach disclaimers that add that this is only an *estimate*. Indicate clearly that the actual award may differ slightly and the early estimator may not include institutional funds based on academic merit. Hopefully, this would prompt the family to seek further information and allow the admission counselor to discuss merit scholarships and other financing options with the family. Offer the service to all prospects if your market position indicates that it would be most useful at this stage in the college decision process. Make this available to prospective students who have actually applied for enrollment if your school's marketing position indicates that it would be most effective at that point in the college decision process. If you use the early estimator, be certain that its results are tracked and analyzed and understood by all members of the enrollment management team. If you used an early estimator and were not pleased with the results, go back to the drawing board and find out what went wrong. Ask your student-customers who used the service to evaluate it. Learn from them how to improve it and try again. I think it's worth it.

STUDENT DEBT

In 1985 I wrote my first book on college financing called *Mortgaged Futures: How to Graduate from School Without Going Broke*. The book's main theme was that college students were borrowing too much money and planning too little on how they would repay their student loan bills or how their student debt would affect their careers and future lives. I could not find a publisher because I was told student debt was not a problem. So I published the book myself and sold over 20,000 copies to colleges, universities, libraries, and higher administration organizations who believed it was a problem. Today, there are national conferences and large consulting firms which specialize in the issues and concerns of student debt.

According to the report "College Debt and the American Family," published by the Education Resources Institute and the Institute of Higher Education Policy, students and their families borrowed almost $30 billion in 1995 and are likely to borrow more than $50 billion per year by the year 2000. About 15 million students use student loans to finance at least part of their education. Recent changes in federal financing policies have contributed to more students borrowing more money to finance their education. Failure of federal loan programs to keep pace with rising tuition rates and a shift from grant allocation to loan allocation has resulted in an explosion in borrowing and student debt. There are many projections and implications of borrowing too much. (I once heard of a graduate student who told her boyfriend that before considering marriage she wanted to see the results of his blood test and his promissory notes!)

We should consider student debt within the context of other types of borrowing. We are a nation of borrowers. Our national debt continues to skyrocket each year as do most types of consumer debt. (Current consumer debt is estimated to be about $1 trillion.) It has become more than acceptable to borrow for college, and although I believe that because of escalating college costs, borrowing will be a *part* of most students' financial aid packages, I am concerned about the increased level of borrowing.

However, the jury is out on exactly how much a student should borrow or what is manageable or unmanageable debt. There are no definitive national studies on the implications of debt on the next generation, and those studies that have been completed report on graduates, not on students who withdrew from school, who never graduated, and who owe money. Many college and university administrators do not know how much their students are borrowing and few schools have intensive and aggressive (and I use these words positively) debt counseling programs. Many college students who borrow have given little thought as to how this will affect their future lives. I know of several college graduates who, after graduation, returned to their parents' home to pay off their college debts and who have delayed purchasing a car or other consumer items because they felt they could not afford them.

The dictionary defines the word *projection* as a calculation of something. The following are my projections, of some of the possible long-term consequences of unmanageable student debt.

Postponement of the "Good Life"

Recent national surveys indicate that for many college students finding meaningful and financially rewarding employment after graduation is one of the main reasons for attending college. Upward mobility and discretionary income was once considered the expected outcome of a college diploma. Graduates who must postpone purchasing some of the consumer items that they have come to consider not luxuries, but rather necessities, may feel cheated by their college education. Many college graduates have an unclear notion of what financial shape their lives will take after graduation. However, if the reality of the present does not match expectations of the future, a feeling of helplessness may occur. If strapped by unmanageable student debt, some graduates may fail to realize the return on their college investment that they had come to expect.

Getting Deeper into Debt

In his book *Inequality in an Age of Decline*, sociologist William Blumberg reports that borrowing in this country has come to be considered a natural way to conduct one's financial affairs. Many young people, he writes, do not have the same regard for hard work and savings as their parents or grandparents had. Some college students treat their college education like a mortgage. Postsecondary education has come to be regarded by some as another consumer item to be financed and paid for from future earnings. But how much is too much? And how can student debt be incorporated into other consumer debt so that monthly payments are manageable? No one has the answers to these questions. However the fact remains that more students are borrowing more money to finance their college educations.

Postponement of Marriage and Children

There is some anecdotal evidence to suggest that some college graduates with high debt burdens are willing to delay marriage and starting a family until they have established themselves professionally and financially. More and more college graduates are returning home after graduation in order to save money and pay off student loans. The demographics of the next decade could be quite different from what they are today if these trends continue.

Shift in National Attitude Toward Higher Education

The majority of Americans still believe in the value of a college education. However, the recent changes in the federal government's funding policies sends a message to young people: Borrow for your education. The federal government is no longer able or willing to finance higher education the way it once did with generous grants and low cost loan programs.

Decline in Graduate School Enrollment

Some college graduates, already burdened by a sizable undergraduate student debt, may decide to delay or forego graduate school. There are even fewer grants available for graduate students than for undergraduates. In some graduate programs, engineering and the sciences, for example, there is evidence of a substantial decline in the number of American students and an increase in the number of international students enrolled in those majors.

Shift in Preferred Majors

Several surveys of freshmen indicate that for many, being able to find a job after graduation and earning a high salary are reasons for enrolling in college. Higher education is viewed as a means to an end, and that end often revolves around getting a well paying job. There is nothing wrong with this except when a student selects a college major based only on future income. Carnegie survey data suggest that some undergraduates do not pursue majors in their field of primary interest. Rather, they enroll in programs which hold the promise of high salaries in the future.

Increase in Student Employment

While there is no national study to support this opinion, I believe that more students are working more hours to help meet their college expenses. There is nothing wrong with working. Many of you reading this book probably had a part-time job while you were a college student. I remember my days working in the Registrar's Office at St. John's University in New York. I worked fifteen hours every week and that was my spending money. I can't think of any of my friends that did not have some part-time job. However, some of today's college students are working much longer hours and are using the money earned to help meet their tuition bills. There is evidence to suggest that full-time students working more than 25 hours per week are putting their academic success in jeopardy. The majority of students I have counseled who were on probation were working too many hours. These same students told me that the reason they were working so many hours was their fear of graduating with too much debt. Some decided to take a year off and work full-time. Others dropped from full-time to part-time student status.

I do not believe that events occur in isolation. Nor can change be attributed to a single cause. These projections should be considered within the context of other economic and sociological changes which would impact on the lifestyles and personal career choices of current and future generations of students. However, two things are certain: Students will continue to borrow more and more to meet their financial obligations and colleges and universities must respond with effective debt counseling and debt management programs.

WHERE TO BEGIN AND HOW TO START

If a college or university is serious about establishing a debt management and counseling program, officials at the highest levels must agree that this is a priority and allocate the necessary personnel and financial resources to make the program succeed. Since the financial aid office frequently comes under the supervision of the dean of enrollment, the dean should work with the financial aid office staff to organize the debt management program as part of the division's goals and objectives. If effective, a debt management program can add to a school's marketing, recruitment, and retention programs.

One staff person should be put in charge of organizing the data needed and publishing the necessary debt management materials. Debt management counselors, within the office of financial aid, should make annual loan counseling a part of their overall work assignments. Annual information and debt statistics should be communicated to all members of the campus community.

WRITING AN INSTITUTIONAL FINANCIAL COUNSELING AND DEBT MANAGEMENT PROGRAM

Before writing a debt management program, the following must be known.

- Economic profile of the student body
- Average parental income
- Average parental contribution

- Internal and external sources of funding
- Expected self-help contribution
- Employment opportunities
- Average earnings
- Low cost housing options
- Expected tuition, fees, and housing increases
- Average student indebtedness for freshmen, sophomores, and juniors
- Average indebtedness of graduating seniors
- Impact of debt on student attrition rates
- Job placement at graduation
- Starting salaries in each major

In order to effectively develop a debt counseling and debt management program at your school, assistance is needed from the following.

- Financial aid office
- Budget office
- Data processing office
- Career counseling and placement office
- Registrar's office
- Dean of students office
- Housing office
- Institutional research office
- Retention office

STUDENT COUNSELING

Each student receiving financial assistance should receive at least one hour of financial counseling each year. This is a big commitment of time and personnel, but I believe that in the future, debt counseling will be an intrinsic part of every school's financial aid program. An institutionally approved financial counseling and debt management program should be made available to all future and current students. In counseling sessions, the following information should be exchanged.

1. The student's financial aid award based on the family's income, assets, and contribution
2. The amount of the award that is loan, grant, and employment
3. Monthly living expenses and student budgets
4. The amount of net summer income which can be applied to costs
5. The amount of monthly net income from student employment

6. The number of hours worked each week and the employment location
7. The student's academic profile and grades
8. Career objectives
9. The student's anticipated debt at the time of graduation
10. The repayment terms for all loans
11. The estimated monthly loan payments after graduation
12. Consolidation options
13. The names, addresses, and phone numbers of all lenders
14. Anticipated first year gross and net salary
15. Graduate school enrollment plans and projected additional debt

SOME FINAL THOUGHTS ON STUDENT DEBT

It is the responsibility of the school's financial aid program to counsel students about the sociological, psychological, and financial ramifications of borrowing too much for their undergraduate education. Students should be made aware, ideally before enrollment, of the financial commitments they are likely to incur. The long-term implications of borrowing too much cannot be stressed enough, and both school personnel and individual students and families should work together to seek alternatives to borrowing. Financial aid counselors not only have an obligation to counsel about borrowing too much, but they also have an obligation to counsel school officials about the implications of excessive student debt on the college or university's recruitment and retention programs. Graduation rates will decline if students take fewer courses each semester in order to work more hours. Financial aid directors, in cooperation with the deans of enrollment and retention management, must seek alternative ways for their students to finance their education. The school should commit personnel and financial resources to establish a feasible debt management program which can be realistically administered. Students should be counseled about the financial realities after college. If burdened with unmanageable educational debt, the "good life" may be temporarily or indefinitely postponed. We cannot afford to become a nation where only the rich are educated. We cannot continue to ask the federal government to guarantee unlimited funding levels to all students. We cannot expect that all state governments will be able to replace most federal financial aid dollars with state funds. We should not place undue emphasis on careers with the highest incomes. We should not mortgage the future of the next generation.

11

Retention Management

"If we do not change our direction, we are likely to end up where we are headed."

—Chinese Proverb

Depending on what statistic is quoted, one in every two or one in every three college students will not graduate from the school that he/she entered. Only one student out of every six completes a bachelor's degree in four years. About 40% earn a degree in six years. The national freshman to sophomore dropout rate is almost 30%.

These statistics are discouraging and reflect flaws in the way applicants select schools and schools accept applicants. Are admission counselors, in a frenzy to fill their classes, enrolling anyone, regardless of suitability? Are campus administrators callous to the needs of enrolled students? Something is wrong if so many students fail to graduate from our schools or take five, six, or more years to graduate.

Why are so many students leaving our colleges and universities? In part the answer to this question lies with the type of students who annually enroll in institutions of higher learning. Many of these students could be classified as "non-traditional," that is, underprepared, adult learners, commuters, needing lots of financial aid, borrowing too much, and working too many hours. That's part of the answer but not the entire story. There are other students who are intellectually unchallenged or feel socially isolated. They too are leaving institutions of higher learning. The fact is for the vast majority of colleges and universities, retention is a problem.

Why are students taking longer and longer to graduate? (Remember years ago when we would smile at the athletes who were on "the five-year plan?") A school's first-year attrition rate helps to set the graduation rate for that class. For every student lost, additional pressure is placed on the "front end," the admission office, to replace the students who leave. Also, a satisfied student-customer will speak favorably about his or her college or university. An unhappy student-customer will tell twenty-five people not to go to that school. That certainly will not help the marketing and recruiting programs. It is both ethical and fiscal foolishness not to pay more attention to the retention of our students. It is impossible, in my opinion, to have an efficient and effective enrollment management program without an efficient, effective, and complementary retention management program. At most schools these two functions are separate, often isolated from each other, with different reporting lines and unco-ordinated goals and objectives which may or may not be linked to the overall strategic plan.

At Suffolk University the responsibilities of both enrollment and retention management are combined. We spend as much time retaining students as we do enrolling them. Our marketing and admission programs are based, in part, on the retention program. All prospective students are told before they apply that we are *not* interested in *enrolling* them. We *are* interested in *graduating* them. We recruit *alumni*, not *freshmen*.

There are as many ways to structure a retention management program as there are schools in the country. How it is done and who does it will depend on the same premises that should be used in developing a school's enrollment management program. The campus culture and attrition rates will determine to a great extent how retention management is structured and implemented. The retention program described in this chapter is based on research but is presented in a *practical* way. Like enrollment management, retention management should never be considered finished. There can be no cookie-cutter approach to retaining students. What works at one school may not work at another. However, I believe there are certain aspects of retention management outlined in this chapter which can and will work at most schools. Again, it is my belief that there is not a lot of magic to this. If you genuinely care about retaining students and you develop a responsive system to keep them, if the personnel and resources are allocated to the program, you will be successful.

Consider the Following

- Retention management is *more* important than enrollment management. It is a greater measure of a school's success than enrollment since enrolling in a college or university is just the first step toward fulfilling academic objectives. Also, retention is responsible for 75% of a school's population and tuition revenues.

- Schools spend a great deal of money recruiting and enrolling one quarter of their school and little money on keeping the remaining three-quarters of their population. Many schools do not even know what their attrition rates are. Few college admission counselors know what happens to the students they recruit and enroll. I once listened to the director of admission at a prestigious Ivy League school tell an audience that he didn't know or care about the school's retention rate. It was "someone else's job." Surprisingly, not one person in the audience (including me) challenged this statement. However I felt then, and I believe now, that admission directors have a responsibility to know what happens to the class they recruit. They should know which cohorts of students succeed and which do not.

- The fiscal problems of many schools could be alleviated if more students were retained. Students who drop out after one year represent a loss of the next three years' tuition. If your school's annual tuition is $10,000 and one freshmen stays for all four years, the fiscal return on that student could be as much as $40,000. Even if the student receives institutional funds of $10,000 over the course of four years, the return on the investment is still $30,000. For every student who transfers or drops out after the first year, the net income loss could be as much as $30,000. Multiply that figure by the number of first-year students who withdraw, and the net revenue loss can be substantial.

- Do you know how much it costs to enroll one student? Do you know how much it costs to retain one student?

- It will take at least three years to develop and implement a retention management program. The program should never be finished. As long as you continue to enroll students, new retention challenges will surface.

- One senior level administrator should be in charge of the retention management program and have the authority to implement the necessary changes across the campus. A commitment to support this administrator must come from the president.

- Although based on research, a school's retention management program should be *practical, accountable,* and *flexible.*

- More financial aid will not guarantee higher retention rates. Many students will list financial problems as the main reason for leaving a school. In many cases it's more than that. Feelings that they don't belong, or questioning how to fit into the school environment, and courses that are too challenging or not challenging enough, are more often the underlying reasons for a student's desire to withdraw. Or maybe the applicant and school were not a good fit in the first place.

- Academic underpreparedness may be one of the greatest contributing factors in increased attrition. Although nationally, only about 5% of students are dismissed for academic reasons, many students require remedial work during their first year of college. One recent survey I read indicated that four out of five young adults could not summarize the main point of a newspaper article, read a bus schedule, or figure their change from a restaurant bill. In Boston, 39% couldn't name the six New England states; in Minneapolis and St. Paul, 63% couldn't name all seven continents; in Dallas, 25% couldn't identify the country that borders the United States to the south. Some of these students are enrolled in colleges and universities.

- Retention management cannot succeed without faculty input and advising. A school's greatest attrition weapon is its faculty. Advising is essential to any successful retention management program. Promotion and tenure reviews should *really* consider faculty advising as essential. Good advising should be rewarded and bad or *no* advising should not be tolerated.

- The social life of the campus and a school's student activities are an integral part of a school's retention management program. Student affairs personnel must be brought into the school's retention management program at the time the program is designed.

- A comprehensive list of all retention activities should be disseminated to faculty and staff.

- Institutional retention initiatives should be assessed, evaluated, and changed as needed: every semester or every year.

- The senior administrator in charge of a school's retention management program should meet with all new employees to emphasize their role in retaining students. Last year I was giving a seminar on our program and I mentioned that Maria, a cafeteria worker at Suffolk, did more to retain students than many people at school. Maria makes time for the students. She knows who is struggling in math class and who just broke up with whom. Each student is greeted with a smile that says "I care about you." You are not just a number. You are a person. There is no way to estimate how many people Maria helped retain. There is no doubt that she contributed to the goals of our retention management program. Every administrator and staff person should know what retention management is and the role they can and should play in it.

- Retention management is not about lowering standards, or keeping students in school who should not be enrolled. It may not even be about graduation. Not all of the students you enroll may want to graduate. This will become more apparent in the coming decade as we enroll more adult and part-time students who may want to take courses to upgrade their skills, not earn a degree. Retention management is about assisting each student with reaching his or her educational goal. Each student must decide what that goal is and it many not be a degree.

- Annual retention objectives should be set and agreed upon by faculty and administrators.

- Retention management must begin with solid research to find which students are withdrawing and the reasons for their leaving school as well as a profile of which students persist and why. This information is essential not only for retention management personnel but also for enrollment management staff.

- The courses a school offers, when they are offered and how many courses are required for graduation, play a significant role in retention management. This is particularly important for commuter students and adult learners.

- Research indicates that the first six weeks of the semester are the most critical for retaining first year students as they struggle to adapt to a new environment and academic challenges.

- There must be a synergistic relationship between the deans of enrollment and retention management. Neither can succeed without the other. Retention management is, in many ways, more difficult to achieve than enrollment management. There is no part of the college or university nor member of the campus community that does not have a role in retention and, therefore, it is often more difficult to reach consensus.

- There is no one, right retention management program. A school's program will depend upon the composition of the student body and the reasons why students leave. Some schools have the same retention activities for all students—high-risk students and academically talented students, new freshmen and, transfer students.

- Just as there are different recruitment strategies based on market cohorts, there should also be specific retention strategies for different categories of enrolled students, including:
    —Academically talented students
    —High-risk students
    —Residential students
    —Commuter students
    —Transfer students
    —Athletes
    —Minority students
    —Adult learners
    —Undeclared majors
    —International students
    —Financial aid recipients
    —Graduate students

- Regardless of the college or university, the retention management program must be endorsed by the president. The dean of retention management should have access to the school's president and at least once a semester, should report directly to the president on the program's accomplishments, insights, and challenges.

- Much of the success of a school's retention management program will depend on constructing a program that matches the school's culture and personality, on appointing one person to be responsible and accountable for the program's activities, on allocating money and other necessary resources, and on having a serious commitment to recruiting for graduation and not just admission.

Elements of a Successful Retention Management Program

- Presidential commitment
- One senior level administrator is appointed by the president and given the authority to implement a campus-wide retention management program
- A clear understanding of the student population
- Relevant research on the reasons why students leave and why they persist
- Effective and early intervention techniques
- Caring attitude of faculty and staff
- Reward system for good faculty-student advising
- Frequent assessment of retention activities
- Specific and measurable goals agreed upon by everyone involved
- Retention is considered *more* important than enrollment
- The program matches the school's culture and "personality"

Who Should Play a Role in Retention Management?

- President
- Vice President for Academic Affairs
- Vice President for Finance
- Dean of Retention Management
- Dean of Enrollment Management
- Dean of Students
- Academic Deans
- Departmental Chairpersons
- Admission Director and admission counselors
- Director of Financial Aid and financial aid counselors
- Registrar
- Budget Officer
- Director of Enrollment Research
- Director of Counseling Center
- Director of Learning Resource Center
- Grants Officer
- International Student Advisor
- Director of Minority Student Affairs Director of ESL
- Director of Orientation
- Director of Housing
- Director of Food Service
- Director of Adult and Evening Students
- Director of Computer Center
- Director of Grounds and Maintenance
- Director of Campus Security
- Director of Public Affairs

- Director of Marketing
- Director of Alumni Affairs

Why Is Retention Management So Difficult?

One of the reasons it is so difficult to implement practical and effective retention management practices is that retention management cuts across all campus lines and divisions. It's not possible to have an efficient program without involving most campus personnel. Therefore, the dean of retention management is bound to step on someone's toes. No one wants the responsibility for retention management. However, once someone is given the authority for retention, turf battles can ensue. You can't have a good retention management program without faculty cooperation and input. There may be some faculty who will resent anyone who is put in charge of a program that has academics as essential to its success. Budget officials are more inclined to add fiscal resources to a recruitment program than they are to retention initiatives. Finding and appointing the right person to do the job is difficult. The administrator must have a clear understanding of the school, must be respected and able to work well with people in a non-threatening way, must be resourceful enough to find ways around the systems that are no longer contributing to retention, must be practical and set realistic goals, and must be able to make and implement tough decisions. In short, we are looking for another administrative superstar.

HOW TO BEGIN: A STEP-BY-STEP, PRACTICAL APPROACH TO IMPLEMENTING A RETENTION MANAGEMENT PROGRAM

Phase One: January–May

The president and other senior administrators agree that a retention management program should be implemented at the campus. All agree that the necessary resources, both fiscal and academic, will be allocated to the program.

One senior administrator is hired or selected from within the school community to structure and organize the school's retention management program. The president informs the campus community of the selection of a dean of retention management and makes it clear that this person will be responsible for coordinating all aspects of the school's retention program *and* that the dean of retention management has been given the authority by the president to direct all of the activities of the program.

The dean of retention management should meet with personnel in the office of enrollment research to obtain data on which students are leaving and which are persisting. Student attrition rates, by individual student-cohorts, and academic major, should be obtained. Only after this information is gathered and analyzed will trends become apparent.

The dean of retention management and the director of enrollment research should conduct focus groups of students to get input from their student-customers on what is adding to or subtracting from a healthy retention environment at the school.

A list should be obtained from the registrar's office of all students who left the college or university over the past year. Those students should be contacted by telephone and given the opportunity to indicate why they left the school.

The dean of retention management should meet with the heads of all academic departments to obtain their input on student retention and attrition.

The dean of retention management should meet with all of the key administrators and get their input on student attrition and retention issues.

The dean of retention management should analyze all of the data and make recommendations on what should be changed or what programs and policies need to be added to increase retention rates.

The dean of retention management should present the results of the data analysis to the president and other senior management officials; outline the personnel, academic, and fiscal resources that will be necessary to implement the retention initiatives; and set one, two, and three year goals.

Phase Two: June–August

I never expected to recommend this, but after trying to "go it alone" with retention management and after making every mistake there was to make, I realize that you need a committee to implement a retention management program. Who is on that committee will be determined, to a great degree, by the severity of a school's attrition rates, the results of the data analysis, and the school's culture. At Suffolk, there are twenty members on the retention management committee, and every other year the membership rotates. The same departments are represented on the committee, but the personnel change. This gives everyone an opportunity to learn firsthand of the school's retention initiatives, to have input into the program, and to be a team player. The convening of the retention management committee at Suffolk University has created an opportunity for communication among key campus retention contributors, has decreased unnecessary duplication of effort, and has minimized some of the bureaucratic obstacles to retaining students. The committee has facilitated collaborative thinking and has resulted in an exchange of information and ideas. It has created an opportunity for dialogue among campus administrators and faculty who would not usually engage in close communication about retaining students. Finally, the creation of the retention management committee has provided encouragement to all personnel involved in retaining students.

The dean and committee members should decide on what the committee can realistically accomplish during the first year of the program. Everyone's input and general agreement will be essential at this stage in the program's development.   The summer months should be spent in fine-tuning the program and making necessary policy and programmatic changes.

Phase Three: September–May

Based on research and data analysis, a school's retention management program should be implemented during the fall semester.

The retention program should be evaluated every six months and the results of the evaluation shared with everyone. Every semester, information about the number and category of students who left the institution should be evaluated and compared with previous data. Students who left should be contacted. The reasons for the current semester's attrition may be different from those of previous semesters; and if so, that information will drive the initiatives for the next phase of the retention management program.

The following cohorts of students are likely to need some assistance from a school's retention management program.

- Incoming students with low SAT or ACT scores
- Open or undeclared majors
- Students with a GPA of below 2.0
- Students with poor mid-term grades
- Students with learning disabilities
- Students with frequent absences from class
- Students identified by research as likely to withdraw

FORTY RETENTION MANAGEMENT SUGGESTIONS

The following are retention management suggestions. While *some* may not apply to every student or campus situation, there are some *basic* ideas which I believe can be implemented at most colleges or universities.

1. Retention begins before admission as school and applicant determine if their fit is the right one. Applicants should be given accurate information on the school's admission and financial aid policies and its academic programs. Applicants and their families should be informed about the school's current retention rates, including the rate after the first year and the retention programs that are in place for students who are in academic difficulty.
2. Applicants should be encouraged to attend one or more classes and spend a weekend on campus before enrolling. During this time they should ask a variety of questions, including course scheduling, financial aid, crime on campus, and the availability of faculty for advising. (This information should be obtained from current students and should be compared with the information presented by the admission office. The two should match.) Applicants should go to the library, the dormitory, the cafeteria and ob-

serve. They should listen to current students and reach their own conclusions about the school based on fact and observation. Applicants should also obtain a profile of the school's graduates and should be given names to contact.

3. Faculty advisors should be assigned prior to enrollment, preferably shortly after a deposit is received. Some written or oral contact should occur between the faculty person and the deposited applicant before the May 1 deadline.

4. A survival course should be part of the orientation program. Several years ago we asked Suffolk University's first-year students to tell us what they needed to succeed in the freshman year. The result was a one-week course, offered in the summer, to all incoming students; it included time and stress management techniques, how to listen in class, how to take notes, how to design an appropriate study environment, how to discover one's learning style, how to use the library and the school's computer resources, how to change majors and where to go for help and assistance throughout the university. The course is not mandatory. It should be. Retention rates for students who took the summer program were consistently high. It's effective because our *customers* told us what they needed and because we *listened* to them and designed the program to meet their needs.

5. Students who, after mid-term examinations, are in academic difficulty, should be referred to the learning resource center or should be given special advising and a tutor.

6. Repeated absenteeism should be reported to the dean of retention management and some appropriate intervention should take place.

7. Students listed as undeclared majors should meet with the career counselor. Since research indicates that students with no major leave in a higher proportion than other students, special outreach activities should be planned for this cohort of students.

8. An "early warning system," based on institutional research, should be designed to identify and assist those students who are likely to withdraw. For example, our research indicated that students who still had outstanding tuition balances by a particular point in the first semester were likely to leave. Personal letters were sent to each student in this category and meetings were set up with each student. The first time we tried this, sixty students made appointments. We were able to retain fifty-nine of them. However, in some cases, it was necessary to recommend that the student drop from full-time to part-time status. That was a more reasonable solution for the student and for the university.

9. Each month the dean of retention management should communicate in some way with all new students: freshmen, transfers, and adult learners. This monthly communication can focus on any aspect of the school's retention program that is necessary. The letters or post cards should convey a genuine sense of concern for the student's welfare and success and should provide concrete and practical assistance. For example, students who are

certain they will get a poor or failing grade in a subject should be advised about options for withdrawing from the course. Students with financial problems should be given information on how to appeal for additional aid.

10. Students should be meeting with their advisors prior to pre-registration for the spring semester. Signing course schedules is *not* academic advising. In some "enlightened" schools, pre-registration is administered by personnel in the registrar's office who *really* know about course requirements for graduation and proper course sequencing. Academic and career advising is left to the faculty at another designated time.

11. Students who must withdraw from school should know how to officially and legally do so. Exit interviews should be conducted and the reasons why students leave should be discussed with members of the retention management committee and should become part of the school's retention management's program.

12. Students should know the criteria that would make a difference in their probation or dismissal from school. For example, a student seeking help from the learning resource center or attending special tutoring classes is usually considered favorably by academic standing committees.

13. Someone from the dean of retention management's office should contact all students who do not pre-register for the spring or fall semesters. Information on why these potential "stop-outs" did not register should become part of the school's retention management initiatives.

14. At the end of the first semester, focus groups should be conducted by the dean of retention management and the director of enrollment research. I would recommend using freshmen and junior students in the focus groups. The results of these meetings should be incorporated into a school's retention management program.

15. Personnel from the registrar's office should report to the dean of retention management the attrition and retention statistics for the semester, by student-cohort and by academic department. That information should be shared with the president, senior management, retention management committee members, faculty, and staff. A retention management newsletter should be published highlighting the successes (and failures) of the school's retention program.

16. The dean of retention management should coordinate attrition and retention data each semester from the registrar's office with information from the director of enrollment research. Comparative statistics will indicate progress, or the lack of it, in reaching retention management goals.

17. A tutoring program should be organized and financially supported. Faculty should make frequent and regular referrals for students who are experiencing academic difficulty.

18. An audit should be conducted by personnel in the registrar's office of all students by the end of the sophomore year to be certain they are on track for meeting graduation requirements.

19. Letters of encouragement should be sent by the dean's office to all students on academic probation.

20. Letters of congratulations should be sent by the dean to all students who have been removed from academic probation.

21. Students who must drop from five to four courses because of academic problems should be given a voucher to take one free course in the summer. Families should not be financially penalized by having to pay for a reduced course load. We have such a program at Suffolk, and consistently over 80% of the students who participate in the free summer course program are successful in raising their GPAs.

22. Suffolk initiated a loan program specifically for students who were in academic difficulty. Students are awarded a Presidential Incentive Loan (PIL), and if the student graduates, the loan converts to a grant. This is one way to encourage students to stay in school and graduate.

23. Telecounseling activities should include contacting all first-year students during the first semester. The purpose of the calls is to offer advice to students who need academic assistance or who are experiencing difficulties adjusting to campus life.

24. Frequent consultations should take place between the dean of retention management and the director of the learning resource center. Rosters of students at risk should be cross-referenced.

25. Each academic department should publish a list of departmental retention activities.

26. If research indicates that there is a significant loss of students after the second semester and before the third semester (summer months), outreach activities should be organized and implemented.

27. A master list of students in academic difficulty, students not attending classes, and students who were identified as high-risk should be maintained by the dean of retention management. These lists should be cross-referenced and aggressive and intrusive counseling of all students on the lists, especially those students who appear on more than one list, should be coordinated through the dean's office. The specific format of the counseling and the personnel conducting the counseling sessions will depend upon the number of students involved, how the retention management program is organized, and the financial resources allocated for the program.

28. One staff member from the financial aid office should be assigned to assist first year students with financial aid problems. Students who have not applied for financial aid and who have an outstanding tuition balance should be contacted.

29. The role that a school's financial aid policies play in the retention of students should be continually evaluated. One way to do this is to review and contrast the financial aid awards or the lack of a financial aid package with profiles of students who withdrew. Another way to determine the impact of financial aid on retention is to contact students who withdrew and ask the reasons for their withdrawal. A significant number of students may leave

because they simply cannot afford to attend. The director of enrollment research should work with the director of financial aid to chart trends and interpret data. The result of this analysis should be presented to the dean of retention management who may request a review of certain aspects of the school's financial aid program. The dean of enrollment management should also be given this information as well as the director of admission.

30. A comprehensive advising manual should be written and distributed to all faculty. Input from the entire campus community should be obtained and incorporated into the document.

31. A manual of all of the school's retention activities should be compiled and distributed throughout the campus.

32. Semester attrition reports, by academic unit and department, should be compiled by personnel in the registrar's office and distributed by the dean of retention management. Senior administrative staff, including the president, should be aware of each semester's attrition numbers.

33. A retention newsletter, published each semester, should be written and distributed to the entire campus community by the dean's office.

34. An annual report of the activities and accomplishments of the retention management program should be prepared and distributed throughout the campus community.

35. Every six months the dean of retention management should review the status of the school's retention goals and objectives. If the goals were met, everyone should be informed of this. If they were not, the reasons should be analyzed and changes implemented to bring about the desired outcomes.

36. The dean of retention management should meet with the dean of enrollment management to discuss the results of the data analysis regarding retention. A profile of the students most likely to withdraw, as well as a profile of the persister, should be coordinated with the school's recruitment and enrollment objectives. There should be a clear understanding of who is being retained after enrollment and why. This type of synergy may result in changes to certain aspects of the marketing and recruitment programs.

37. The dean of retention management, in concert with other members of the campus community and with the members of the retention management committee, should determine the goals and objectives of the program for the following year.

38. If appropriate, a school's retention successes should be shared with prospective students and their parents as part of the undergraduate admission marketing plan.

39. Frequent input from the student-customer is essential to any retention management program. Listen to your students. They know why their friends are leaving. No research is more effective than this source.

40. Don't be discouraged if the program cannot respond immediately to what needs to be done. It will take time and a great deal of patience.

SPECIAL ADVISING PROGRAM

At Suffolk University, we have had a Special Advising Program for the past six years. Each year about 300 students, identified as high risk, are assigned to faculty who have been selected to be special advisors. The retention rates for students in this program have ranged from a high of 93% to a low of 85%. In 1994 our Special Advising Program was recognized by the National Academic Advising Association.

Once your research has identified high-risk students, assigning selected faculty to advise these students and tracking them should result in reducing the attrition rate of this cohort of students. To be effective, the program must be based on effective research, use the best faculty as advisors, have sufficient financial resources, and be frequently evaluated and assessed.

Special Advising Program Objectives

- To reduce the attrition rate of identified high-risk students
- To provide formal feedback to students about their academic status early in the semester
- To ensure that the appropriate institutional resources and student services are made available to high-risk students
- To modify the program's implementation and practices whenever necessary
- To adopt effective special advising procedures to other student advising

Program Description

- Every six months the dean of retention management should receive a list of all identified high-risk students. These students should be matched with faculty selected for intensive or special advising. Every attempt should be made to pair faculty with students in their departments or classes. Faculty who have a proven track record of effective advising should be selected to participate in the program. Student evaluations and recommendations from departmental chairpersons should be taken into consideration when selecting faculty for the program.
- The faculty selected for the program should meet with the dean of retention management for a detailed training session, which includes a profile of the students in the program and information from the registrar's office, financial aid office, bursar's office, counseling office, and resource learning center. A handbook of regulations written by personnel in the registrar's office on course sequencing, graduation requirements, re-entry and leave of absence regulations, should be made available to each advisor as should a current advising manual.
- Each faculty member should receive some financial compensation for participating in the program. It may be the salary for teaching one additional course or a percentage of base salary. This compensation will vary from

school to school. The first year we conducted this program, I relied on the good will of a small group of dedicated faculty. However, it soon became apparent that this was too much of a time commitment to ask even the most generous faculty member, and so we gave a $2,500 stipend to the faculty who participated in the program.

- Special advisors should be instructed on what their responsibilities are and what is expected of them each semester. How they conduct their advising sessions should be left up to each advisor and should be a reflection of individual choice and advising style. However, a post-semester assessment of each student should be a program requirement. Feedback to the academic dean's office, as well as the deans of enrollment and retention management, should also be required. Special advisors should provide information on the students they counsel to academic standing committees.

- Transcripts should be provided by the registrar's office and given to each special advisor no later than the first week in the semester. The name of the student's special advisor should become part of the transcript. This information should also be given to the dean of retention management.

- Special advisors should meet weekly with their advisees to discuss course difficulty, class assignments and tutoring opportunities.

- Special advisors should meet monthly as a group to exchange ideas and information about advising students. The program should have the flexibility to accommodate the advising preferences of the faculty and students involved. It is important to give special advisors the freedom and latitude to work with their special advisees as they see fit. While effective advising techniques are shared, they should not be imposed. Since there will probably be a wide diversity in the type of student in the program, no "cookie-cutter" approach will work. Each special advisor should determine which methods work best with the students they are advising.

- Each special advisor should report to the dean of retention management at the end of each semester on the progress and academic standing of each of their special advisees.

- After each semester, statistical data on all of the students involved in the special advising program should be analyzed. Information on how many people withdrew, or were dismissed, should be shared with all special advisors. Necessary changes should be implemented.

- The dean of retention management should meet with any special advisor with consistently low retention rates to determine the cause, and if necessary, the dean may have to replace the advisor.

- At the end of the academic year, all special advisors should meet with members of the retention management committee to exchange ideas and information.

TEN RETENTION REPORTS

The following retention reports should be analyzed each year.

1. Profile of the dropout, including:
   —Entering grades, SAT and ACT scores
   —Transfer students
   —Year in school
   —Major
   —Residential or commuter student
   —Gender
   —Minority status
   —International student
   —Adult learner
   —Graduate student
   —Students receiving financial aid
   —Students not receiving financial aid
2. Profile of the persister, including all of the student cohorts listed above
3. Fall to spring attrition rates by department and school
4. Spring to fall attrition rates by department and school
5. Probation report
6. Leave of absence report
7. Academic dismissal data
8. Stopout report, including students who stopout and re-enroll
9. Withdrawal information
10. Special advisor reports

Basically, retention reports should present a clear profile of the student who is leaving, and why the student is leaving. The reports should indicate the type of student who persists and why. It is important that all of this retention information be discussed with the dean of enrollment management. Are the admission counselors recruiting students who can be successful? Or does the enrollment management program recruit for admission and not graduation? Are the school's financial aid policies a good match for the family income levels of enrolling students? Are students leaving after one semester or one year because they cannot afford to attend?

DEPARTMENTAL RETENTION ACTIVITIES

Although all campus personnel should be retention agents, the caring attitude of faculty is the most potent retention tool. Faculty are on the front line of defense in a school's retention program. Faculty interact with students daily and are largely responsible for guiding their academic programs. Faculty in each department have a responsibility to create for students an environment which allows for student-faculty interaction and in-depth student advising. In addition to faculty advising, there are other activities that can be organized and implemented by academic departments to assist with a school's retention management program.

Retention Activities That Can Be Conducted by Academic Departments for Students in the Major

1. Send personalized letters or call all incoming students *before* they arrive on campus.
2. Publish a newsletter for outlining the latest information on new technology and departmental news.
3. Attempt to match faculty advisors with students who share similar career interests.
4. Sponsor career seminars with guest speakers.
5. Support student clubs and organizations related to the major.
6. Support study groups and tutoring opportunities for students who are in academic difficulty.
7. Prepare a departmental course planning guide detailing all requirements for graduation and suggested course sequences.
8. Monitor students with incomplete grades.
9. Sponsor receptions and social gatherings to enhance program identity.
10. Develop an alumni mentoring program.
11. Agree to limit class size for introductory courses, whenever possible.
12. Identify internship opportunities and other career-related employment for students in the major.
13. Provide course evaluation forms to students and revise curriculum to address student concerns about course relevancy, timeliness of course offerings, and manageability of graduation requirements.
14. Sponsor a special event for students who graduate in the major.
15. Spend long and patient hours advising!

ADVISING HANDBOOK

When I first began organizing the retention activities at Suffolk University a faculty member told me that he did not know how to advise because there was no handbook. So we wrote one and distributed it to all full-time and part-time faculty.

Advising Handbook Should Have the Following Information

Resource Directory—listing of the names, locations, and phone numbers of personnel in the admission offices, learning resource center, bookstore, campus ministry, career services, counseling center, academic deans' offices, deans of enrollment and retention management, dean of students, residence life office, financial aid office, health services office, housing office, international programs office, multicultural affairs office, physical plant, registrar's office, student accounts office, student activities department, university police, vice presidents' offices and the office of the president.

Departmental Chairpersons—listing the names, locations, and phone numbers of each departmental chairperson.

University Calendar—listing important dates and deadlines in each academic semester.

Advising Process—listing the purposes of the academic advising program and the responsibilities of the faculty advisor.

Common Problems—listing frequent problem situations, including information on how to drop or add a course, change a major, course sequencing, converting incomplete grades to letter grades, and where to refer students with financial problems, learning disabilities, housing or health concerns.

General Information—listing information on school policy about class cancellations, classroom attire, drug and alcohol policies of the school, sexual harassment policies, smoking regulations, and student conduct issues.

University Services—listing information about the library, the cafeteria, and university police, the computer center, the media center, the copy center, and so on.

Student Services—listing information on campus ministry, career services, counseling center, dean of students office, disability services for students, health services, housing information, residence life, international programs, learning resource center, minority student support services, and veterans' services.

Student Organizations—listing the names, locations, and phone numbers of all student clubs and organizations.

Admission Information—listing acceptable grades and test scores as well as readmission information.

Tuition Information—listing tuition per course and per semester as well as mandatory fees, alternative methods of payment and tuition liability and student withdrawal from classes.

Financial Aid Information—listing important dates and deadlines for filing financial aid forms, the school's financial aid policies and appeal procedures, and a list of the college or university's financial aid programs.

General Education Information—listing information on absenteeism, declaring a major, academic standing regulations, probation, change of grade policy, change of major policy, cheating and plagiarism, final examination policy, grading system, graduation requirements, late registration procedures, outside course requests, petition for waiver of degree requirement, procedure for appealing grades, the registration process, repeating a course regulations, leave of absence policy, and student withdrawal from school.

The advising manual or handbook should be updated each year and distributed to all departments by the dean of retention management. It can and should serve as a tool in faculty advising and give advisors the ability and confidence to answer most questions about school policies.

Retention management will succeed if the president supports the program and the entire campus community considers keeping students more important than enrolling them. To be successful a school's retention program should have one administrator responsible for the overall administration of the program. The necessary financial resources should be allocated and research should indicate which high risk students would most benefit from early and effective intervention techniques. Finally, to be successful any retention management program should match the school's culture.

Expect resistance. No one wants to manage retention. However, the minute someone is put in charge, turf battles begin. Be realistic. Set targeted goals and don't be discouraged by all that still needs to be done. Stick to your agenda. Know what you want to initiate and why. Be flexible. If something comes up that should be immediately addressed, adjust the agenda to accommodate the issue. Try not to get frustrated or overwhelmed. Remember, in order to change a school's retention rate, it is necessary to change group behavior. That's not an easy thing to do.

Get student input. Students will tell you why they left and why they stay. Listen to your customers. Celebrate your success with everyone on campus. Make everyone feel a part of the retention management program. Publish annual statistics, and see that the information is presented to the president and other senior administrators. Avoid shortcuts at all cost. Tailor your program to your student population. Each school should and will have a different program. There is really not a lot of magic to retaining students. While it is nearly impossible to keep all of the students we enroll, we can and should be keeping more than we are. If you treat your student-customers well, if you make students feel that their academic success is important, they will respond. Remember, happy graduates make good alumni!

It is no accident that retention management is the longest chapter in this book. Since combining the enrollment and retention management activities at Suffolk University, a single, transparent system of enrolling students and then helping them to achieve their academic objectives, has become reality. Admission is just the first step in a student's success and in our role in the life of that student. I don't know how we could separate effective recruitment activities from effective retention initiatives. At Suffolk, the two programs are so tightly woven together that the successes or failures in one program have immediate and tangible effects on the other.

In 1993 our program was cited by Noel Levitz as one of the best overall retention programs in the country. In 1994 Suffolk University was named by Barron's Publishing Corporation as one of the "300 Best College Buys." One of the reasons for the selection was the comments from students about the university's retention program and its commitment to students. In one way these external awards validated our internal retention activities and allowed everyone who contributed to the program to be part of its success.

The chart on the following page illustrates how the Retention Management Program was organized at Suffolk University.

RETENTION MANAGEMENT PROGRAM

Organization Chart

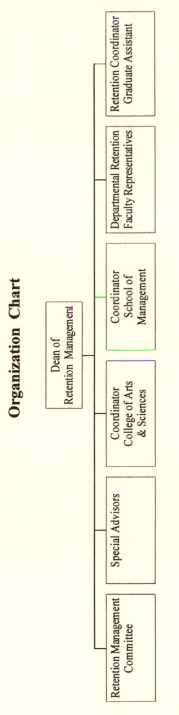

Dean of
Retention Management

Retention Management
Committee

Special Advisors

Coordinator
College of Arts
& Sciences

Coordinator
School of
Management

Departmental Retention
Faculty Representatives

Retention Coordinator
Graduate Assistant

12

Outcomes

"American colleges and universities hold one central goal in common: to help students learn. Rarely, however, do institutions attempt to discover whether or how much their students are learning."

—Principles of Accountability of Colleges and Universities

Not long ago, I had a conversation with Robert Morse, the reflective and belea-guered director of data analysis for *U.S. News & World Report's* America's Best Colleges. We discussed how he compiled the data for the survey and how the information was tabulated. During the course of that conversation I asked Mr. Morse if he ever considered compiling a very different kind of survey—a survey of outcomes. Instead of listing data on entrance requirements, endowment per student, and so on, this publication would focus on what happened to students after admission, enrollment, and graduation. I don't know whether Robert Morse or anyone else will ever compile this information, but I, for one, would be interested in reading the results.

There is a growing trend in this country for colleges and universities to be held accountable, even to guarantee a student's "success" after graduation. Increasing college costs are making parents from all economic backgrounds ask what they are getting for their tuition dollars. Legislators and governing boards are asking the same kinds of questions and have the same accountability issues. However illogical it may seem to hold a college or university partially accountable for a person's success in life, I don't think this trend is likely to go away any time soon. Nor should it. People want to know that their higher education experience is preparing them or their children to lead productive lives after graduation. These questions have the right to be asked and answered.

Recently I read an article about Henry Ford Community College in Dearborn, Michigan, which gives this guarantee: it will offer its graduates up to sixteen semester hours of further training if an employer indicates that the graduate lacks the technical job skills expected for an entry level job. Rockland Community College in Suffern, New York, initiated a program called Contract for Learning Assurance. This program promises unlimited remedial instruction for students if they succeed in earning a degree but fail to adequately perform certain basic skills. St. John Fisher College in Rochester, New York, gives up to $5,000 in refunds to students who are unable to find a job within six months of graduation. The Milwaukee School of Engineering in Wisconsin, the University of the Pacific, Dominican College in California, Depauw University, the University of Montana, the University of Iowa, and Indiana University-Bloomington, all have adopted a policy that guarantees students a degree in four years provided they meet certain requirements.

What is this all about? When was it established that there were certain rights which automatically came with a college diploma? What about the value of a liberal arts education being something quite sacred and separate from job placement? The tension between the two prevailing opinions—education for its own sake and higher education as the ticket necessary for a good job—have been around for a long time and will not go away any time in the future. I think it is also reasonable and desirable for college administrators to want to know what happens to the students they educate and graduate. How can we make our programs and processes better unless we have our student-customers evaluate us? Rather than view this as threatening, higher education administrators should consider the evaluation process as an opportunity to learn and grow from the students we educate.

There are several methods of gathering information on graduates. I will focus on three: an exit survey of graduates, a job placement report, and an alumni census.

GRADUATING STUDENT EXIT SURVEY

Each year as students complete their education and apply for graduation, information should be gathered from them about the college or university, its educational programs, and how students perceived the services offered by the school.

Survey Questions Should Include

- Gender
- Racial or ethnic description

- Age
- Academic major
- Part-time or full-time status
- Day or evening student
- Enrolled as a freshman, transfer, or graduate student
- Citizenship status
- Year of matriculation
- How time was spent when not attending classes
- Number of hours worked each week and where
- Rating the faculty
- Rating the advising program
- Course availability
- Level of satisfaction with educational experience
- Willingness to serve as a class agent or recruit students
- Evaluation of services and programs, including admission, registration, financial aid, library, cafeteria, athletic program, bookstore, computer facilities, counseling center, health services, student activities programs, student accounts office, learning resource center, academic departments, and the dean of students' office.
- Open-ended questions allowing the graduates the opportunity to indicate what they liked most and least about the school and what they plan to do after graduation.

The results of the graduating senior exit survey should be published. The president, academic and administrative vice presidents, faculty, and the deans of enrollment and retention management should evaluate their respective programs in light of what their graduating student-customers indicated. After this information is obtained, programs and services should be reviewed. Any necessary changes should be implemented. The entire campus community should receive the survey results, and these annual evaluations should be compared each year. Finally, if the information is positive, it should be given to prospective applicants and their families. If the information is not positive, change what needs to be changed.

JOB PLACEMENT REPORT

At more and more information sessions parents and applicants ask about the kinds of jobs our graduates get after they leave Suffolk. Fortunately, parts of our admission publications include information on job placement. You will need the assistance of the career services office or whatever other office of your school is charged with compiling job placement data of graduates to incorporate this information as part of the admission program. A summary of graduates who are working, average salary by major, types of employment, names of employers and graduates enrolled in graduate and professional schools should all be part of the information that is compiled and annually published. This data should be shared with the entire enrollment management division, especially with the admission counselors. If this information is positive, it should be given to prospective applicants and their families.

ALUMNI CENSUS

Working with staff in the alumni office, information about graduates should be obtained every few years from alumni. The results of the alumni survey can and should be used by all campus constituencies. This information is particularly important to the deans of enrollment and retention management because it presents data on what happens to a school's graduates and this information can be shared with prospective applicants and their families.

The Alumni Census Should Ask the Following

- Name
- Address
- Title and profession
- Ethnic origin
- Degree, year of degree, major
- Highest degree attained
- Personal and professional affiliations
- Employer's name and address
- Spouse's name, college or university attended, profession, and title
- Names and ages of children
- Other family members who attended the college or university
- Willingness to recruit students or serve on alumni boards
- Reasons for attending this college or university
- School's role in preparation for future career
- Rate the quality of the education
- Most influential faculty, administrator, or staff person
- Participation in alumni events
- Willingness to assist with fundraising activities
- Best and worst thing about the school
- General attitude toward the school

Like the graduating senior survey information and the job placement results, if this information is positive, it should be made available to prospective applicants and their families. If the information received from graduates is not positive, someone should determine how best to respond to the alumni's concerns.

How exactly does one measure student learning and success? There is no one test that can assess these things. There is no single method that would apply to all schools and disciplines. Everyone learns in a different way. Nevertheless, to ignore the issue is no longer acceptable. The parents who pay the tuition bills, the citizens who support public institutions, and the employers who hire employees with poor reading and writing skills and then must re-train or educate them, are demanding accountability.

Higher education administrators should want to assess what they do and how they deliver their educational product to their customers. They should want to receive a report card from their current and past students. How did we educate our students? What impact did the school have on their lives? How did we prepare them for work or graduate school? How do they feel about the way they were treated as students? What are the feelings about their "alma mater" after graduation? What is the perceived value of their educational experience?

Institutional self-analysis and assessment is essential in any organization. Can deans of enrollment and retention management really do their jobs without information from their current students and alumni? Every president, provost, alumni director, and faculty member should want to have feedback on how to make the educational experience for their students both meaningful and relevant.

SOME FINAL THOUGHTS

The following are some of the questions frequently asked by parents and applicants. I believe these are questions that the higher education community will continue to be asked in the future.

- Why does tuition frequently increase more than the consumer price index?
- Why is the academic year shorter than it once was?
- What about "truth-in-advertising"? Is the marketing message based in reality? Is the information in admission publications accurate?
- What role does remedial education have in higher education?
- Is the curriculum relevant? Who determines that relevancy?
- What is the minimum competency that every student should have at graduation?
- How are colleges and universities preparing their students to compete in a global economy?
- How is the college or university preparing itself to meet the challenges of the next century?

These are not *my* questions. These are the questions I am frequently asked by our customers—parents, applicants, students, and alumni. I believe that the questions, or the climate which encourages them, will not go away now or in the near future. All of us in higher education will and should be held accountable for the way we manage our businesses and conduct our professional lives. The public has a right to ask these questions and to receive credible answers. No longer can higher education administrators operate under the illusion that they know best. None of us is above having to respond, in a credible way, to the demands and questions of the constituencies we serve.

13

Evaluation

"Universities must monitor what they are supposed to do."

— Alexander Austin

Sophisticated computer systems, excellent data analysis and a dedicated staff are all essential ingredients for a successful enrollment and retention management program. However, without careful reflection and frequent evaluation, a school's program may not achieve the desired results. A built-in evaluation system, for each facet and phase of all programs, must be part of the overall system. In fact, it should drive the enrollment and retention management objectives and dictate what should be kept, what should be modified, and what should be dropped from the programs. Marketing audits, image analysis, publications and advertising checks, research-driven surveys of our student-clients, information on customer satisfaction and dissatisfaction, and careful analysis of which students a school is losing or keeping should be a part of any evaluation system. All staff members should know that their part in the process will be measured for effectiveness and that they will be held accountable. If any part of the program is not contributing to the desired outcomes, it should be reviewed, changed, or eliminated and new approaches initiated.

Evaluation is a constant process, but a formal review should take place every three to six months. Changes that can or need to be made immediately should be. This process allows the deans of enrollment and retention management to make timely decisions *during* the recruitment and academic year instead of *after* the year is over.

Aspects of Enrollment and Retention Management Programs That Should Be Regularly Evaluated for Effectiveness

1. Admission strategy and initial contact with information sources
2. Home page information
3. Media presentations
4. Advertisements
5. Publications
6. High school visits, college fairs, college visits, corporate outreach events
7. Information sessions and accepted student receptions
8. Campus visit programs
9. Interview process
10. Telecounseling program
11. Faculty contact with prospective, accepted, and enrolled students
12. Admission process
13. Financial aid process
14. Registration process
15. Orientation programs
16. Residence hall experience
17. Net tuition policy
18. New student enrollment analysis
19. Total student enrollment analysis
20. Enrollment in all programs and all departments—comparative data
21. Full-time and part-time students—comparative data
22. International student enrollment—enrollment vs. countries visited
23. Minority student enrollment
24. Non-degree student enrollment
25. Top sending high schools, transfer schools, colleges and universities
26. SAT, ACT scores data analysis
27. GMAT, GRE, and other similar data analysis
28. GPA comparative data analysis
29. Demographic analysis
30. Psychographic analysis
31. Yield rates
32. Enrollment by gender
33. Non-matriculating student enrollment—comparative data
34. Enrollment projections
35. Early financial aid estimator analysis
36. Institutional financial aid awards and enrollment yields
37. Enrollment yields and timing of financial aid award
38. Federal grant and loan comparative data

39. State grant and loan data
40. Unmet need analysis
41. Average financial aid award
42. Average family income of students receiving financial aid
43. Average family income of students not applying for financial aid
44. Non-matriculating students and financial aid award
45. Competitor schools' financial aid awards—comparative data
46. Gross vs. net tuition revenues
47. Average loan indebtedness
48. Student employment statistics
49. Financial aid recipients and retention statistics
50. Financial aid recipients and graduation statistics

Retention Evaluation
51. Overall retention rate—comparative data
52. Undergraduate retention rate—comparative data
53. Graduate student retention rate—comparative data
54. Non-degree student retention rate—comparative data
55. Minority student retention rate—comparative data
56. International student retention rate—comparative data
57. Stopout data analysis
58. Official leave of absence data analysis
59. Official withdrawal data analysis
60. Academic dismissal data analysis
61. Attrition rates data analysis
62. Graduation rates—comparative data
63. Retention rates by year in school
64. Academic advising and retention/attrition analysis
65. Special advising and effectiveness of tutor programs
66. Course section and selection analysis
67. Course withdrawal data analysis
68. Course failure data analysis

Staff Evaluation
69. Staff input and evaluation of enrollment and retention management programs
70. Evaluation by the deans of enrollment and retention management of all staff

Even if a school's enrollment and retention management programs are both efficient and effective, evaluating all of the major facets of the programs is a difficult and complicated undertaking. However, it is an absolutely essential one. Do you remember what Lewis Carroll had Alice ask of the Cheshire cat: "Would you please tell me which way I ought to go from here?" Do you remember the response? "That depends on where you want to get to."

The best deans of enrollment and retention management won't know where to take their programs or how to take their programs to the next level without careful analysis and thoughtful and frequent evaluation. To conduct this activity,

the deans must have the input and cooperation of all of the directors in the divisions and should rely heavily on the director of enrollment research for data col-
lection and analysis. Based on the information obtained, activities should be
dropped, modified, or added to make the marketing, enrollment, retention, and
graduation of students the most effective and efficient that it can be. No small
task, but it can be done!

14

Success and Failure

"Go on failing. Go on. Only next time, try to fail better."

— Samuel Beckett

Despite the best and most creative efforts of enrollment and retention managers and despite the best evaluation processes, implementing effective programs may fail. There are several reasons for this.

A lack of *presidential commitment* can only result in failure. Many presidents expect an instant turnaround if they put more personnel or money into the admission budget, or hire a public relations firm to fix the school's image problem. This mentality can only result in a lack of understanding of the real reasons for a school's enrollment decline and in the unwillingness to seek a more global, long-term solution to the institution's enrollment and retention management problems. However, if a president or chief executive officer fails to realize the reasons behind a school's enrollment decline or high attrition rates, the enrollment and retention managers may have failed to present an accurate and realistic analysis of the situation or may have failed to present viable solutions to the problems. The deans of enrollment and retention management must have a clear mandate from the president to direct the school's enrollment and retention programs. This mandate should be articulated to the entire campus community so that there is no confusion over the deans' responsibilities.

The *inappropriate* selection of the dean or deans of enrollment and retention management is a sure recipe for disaster. I have known several enrollment and retention managers who have designed what appears to be effective and efficient enrollment and retention management programs, only to leave their school after a short time in frustration and disillusionment. Some of these colleagues were, in my opinion, good researchers but not dynamic leaders. Or they were dynamic leaders without having a clear understanding of the school's culture. Others were poor managers of people. They could not inspire their staffs or convince skeptical faculty of the benefits of new programs.

Inadequate planning or no planning will make it impossible for any enrollment or retention management program to succeed. Inherent in this design flaw is the lack of pertinent research which can and should direct all enrollment and retention management activities.

The inability to *articulate* and *communicate* effectively and convincingly to the campus community about the school's current enrollment and retention problems or to convince in a persuasive and non-threatening way, how these problems could be managed and solved can only result in confusion and misunderstanding. I have just recently learned of one university which has the personnel department report to the dean of enrollment management. All new employees are trained in the value of customer service and what their role is in retaining students. This is a unique staff reporting structure and one that could be very effective.

Poorly designed and non-integrated programs cannot succeed. An enrollment management program that begins and ends in the undergraduate admission office, or one that fails to consider retention management as part of its overall system, is only half as effective as a system which treats both enrollment and retention management as one integrated and synergistic system. Programs based on instincts or intuition or programs based solely on research are also likely to fail.

A program which excludes *academic programs and faculty* input cannot be successful. Admission counselors can only sell what a school has to offer. If a school's academic programs don't meet the needs of its customers, or if courses are offered at the wrong time, no amount of "selling" will increase enrollment. A retention management program with little or poor faculty academic advising cannot meet with success. All of the research indicates that faculty are the most effective retention managers a school has. These are the men and women who, on a daily basis, affect the lives of the student-customers. No retention management program can compensate for poor teaching or lack of faculty advising.

A lack of adequate *financial resources* will doom any program to failure. It is the job of enrollment and retention managers to gather data on how much it costs to enroll one student at the college or university and how much is spent on retaining students. Enrollment and retention managers must have reasons for requesting funds to implement their programs and should be able to articulate what the return on that investment will be with increased enrollment and retention rates.

Looking for a *quick fix* is not the same as implementing an effective system. Depending on the nature and scope of a school's enrollment and retention problems, it may take from three to five years to put into place all of the systems and programs necessary to implement an enrollment and retention management program. These are incremental and evolutionary programs, works in progress. As long as there are changes taking place in higher education, enrollment and retention management deans should continually review all aspects of their programs and initiate change when necessary.

Inadequate *time* to conduct necessary research and planning will contribute to the programs' failure. For the past several years I have spent one day a week away from the office to think and do research. When I first mentioned this to colleagues, they smiled and asked what I really did on my "day off." All I can tell you is that this time, devoted to careful planning and analysis, has produced some of the most creative and innovative aspects of the enrollment and retention management programs initiated at Georgetown and Suffolk University. You cannot conduct this kind of activity if you are racing from one meeting to the next, are continually answering the phone, or responding to the fax machine or your e-mail messages.

Lack of *focus and inability to delegate* will contribute to an inefficient program. Several years ago I asked my assistant to track all of the meetings I attended each month. She also categorized the meetings. We were both amazed to learn that the number of meetings for one academic year exceeded 600. (This was part of the "only I can fix it syndrome.") This exercise told me that I needed to delegate more effectively, needed to use the phone more efficiently, and perhaps, at times, needed to just say no.

Little or no *interaction* between enrollment and retention management will result in limited success in both programs. Even at institutions that have an enrollment management system, it is rare to have enrollment management tightly integrated with retention management. We have experienced many advantages of combining the two programs at Suffolk University. All of our marketing and recruitment plans include information about the retention management program. Our retention efforts on behalf of our students are marketed to prospective students and their families as a *benefit*. Combining enrollment and retention management allows a school to study the profile of the drop-out and the persister and can relate that information with recruitment markets, and admitted students. Admission counselors can be given a profile of which students are most likely to be successful and which are likely to withdraw. I realize this system and reporting structure is unique and would not work at many colleges and universities because of their size, culture or internal politics. However it is structured, the two programs should be integrated and should complement each other. If there are two deans, they should work closely to achieve the school's enrollment and retention goals.

If the programs' activities are improperly *evaluated*, it will be impossible to adequately assess success or failure. It is tedious and can be threatening to continually evaluate what you are doing, but this is an essential ingredient in enrollment and retention management. Frequent analysis will tell you if you are doing the right things and if you are doing the right things right.

If *change* is introduced too rapidly without regard for the personnel affected or the campus culture, it will be difficult (impossible) to implement a new order of things. No matter how antiquated the programs or how difficult the personnel, the deans must respect what preceded them and work within the established norms. Change should be incremental and there should be a justifiable reason which has been communicated to everyone involved. This is a very common pitfall. A new and energetic dean will try to do it all and often will stampede anyone or anything in the way. It never works. We all need people to make our enrollment and retention programs come alive. We cannot do it alone, even with a clear mandate from the president.

If you try to do it all yourself, *burnout* will most certainly result. As I indicated earlier in this book, I have made every mistake there is to make. One of my biggest errors was being a workaholic and thinking I could do it all. It never occurred to me that working ten-hour days, six days a week, and not taking any time off, was making me less, not more, efficient. I used to think that if I worked harder, more students would come to the university and a greater number of them would stay. I realize now that I alone am not responsible for solving every enrollment and retention problem there is. Feeling tired, resentful, and frustrated are not the qualities of innovative leadership. Taking time off, spending time with your family, and learning how to relax will make you a nicer person and a better manager. Remember, no one on their deathbed ever wished that they had gone to more meetings!

15

Change: Our Constant Companion

"Asking a college to quickly change its approach is akin to asking an ocean liner to make a quick right in the middle of the Atlantic Ocean."

—Dr. Ernest Boyer

In an article in "The Futurist," Daniel Yankelovich writes about the early stages of what psychologists call a "working through" process. This process is defined as the need to reconcile conflict and disappointment created by the need to adapt to change. The struggle manifests itself in demonstrations of anger, confusion, panic, overreaction, exaggeration, depression, fatalism, grasping at straws, and scapegoating.

Does this describe the enrollment and retention situation in higher education today? Are we in a "working through" process? How do we deal with the decline in applicants, escalating tuition costs, maintaining academic standards, technological advances, changes in federal and state funding, and a public who is demanding accountability? Do higher education administrators consider enrollment and retention management a challenge, an insurmountable problem or a change from what was the "way we always did it" to a new paradigm?

In the book, *Reinventing the University Managing and Financing of Higher Education*, each of the fourteen contributors emphasize that the successful university of the future will be the one which has the capacity to create new structural paradigms which will direct how it conducts business and how it delivers its educational product. This newly structured enterprise will be both seamless and transparent in the systems used to deliver services to its student-customers. The university of tomorrow will be marked by different functions and reporting structures from the ones which exist today. It will constantly and consistently focus on the "macro" and pay less attention to the "micro." It will follow a strategic plan which is both understood and embraced by the entire campus community.

I am including a chapter on change in this book because I believe that change is extremely important and is often unrecognized as one of the necessary and essential ingredients in any school's successful enrollment and retention management programs. Without a universal willingness and acceptance of change and without an environment that welcomes and embraces change, the best programs will be unsuccessful. Some may argue that this is a chapter of cliches, of stating the obvious. However, I have observed and know of many enrollment and retention management programs that have failed because insufficient time was given to preparing personnel to deal with both the inevitability and consequences of change. I have many colleagues, talented and dedicated women and men, who are simply worn out asking the "ocean liner to make a quick right in the middle of the Atlantic Ocean."

Sometimes when I have conducted enrollment and retention management workshops I felt negative vibrations among some of the participants. Perhaps there was resentment that an outside "expert" was hired to suggest how to improve the school's enrollment and retention programs. (I always begin by telling people that I am not a consultant, and that I have made every mistake there is to make.) What I am really sensing is people's reactions to change and fear— fear that they will lose their jobs or will feel uncomfortable doing their jobs in a different way.

How often I heard the following:

1. It won't work here. We tried it once.
2. We have always done it this way.
3. It will cost too much.
4. Don't fix it if it's not broken.
5. We don't have the time.
6. We don't have the staff.
7. Let's form a committee.
8. You don't understand.
9. It's not my job.
10. It feels too uncomfortable.

To my ears, these are more than simple, declarative sentences. To me these sentiments symbolize an underlying fear at many colleges and universities today: fear about creating new markets, or strengthening old ones. Fear about enrollment yields and attrition rates. Fear that accountability really means being blamed or fired when targets are not met. Fear that no matter what is done it will never be enough. Fear of changing the way we do our work and view our student-customers.

Change at any college or university affects everyone, including trustees, the president, senior administrators, middle managers, support staff, faculty, students, and alumni. Each of us brings to our offices our own set of beliefs and insecurities. Change makes everyone feel uncomfortable. Change involves setting different rules, making people's work environment uncertain, unpredictable, and therefore, stressful. Change represents loss.

Few organizations change willingly. Usually market forces or customers demand change. Certainly this is true in higher education. We all know of offices in our schools where students are still treated as an annoyance, an interruption and not as valued clients. We all know of employees who no matter what, will never change the way they view themselves, their work, and the students they are supposed to serve.

For enrollment and retention management programs to succeed, it is necessary that change become everyone's constant companion. Every school has its unique culture and "personality," with mores that indicate that it is acceptable to behave in a certain way. If that culture is contributing to the successful enrollment and retention of students, then leave it alone. If that is not the case, and that campus culture is not contributing to a successful program, then it's time to initiate constructive change.

Before an enrollment and retention manager can initiate change, it is necessary to build people's comfort levels. Staff must feel free to fail, to take risks and not be penalized if activities do not produce the desired results. How can you create a climate for change? First, the enrollment and retention manager, by the very nature of their work, are change agents. This must be recognized and valued and have the support of the highest levels within the school, including the president. Secondly, the reasons for change have to be carefully articulated to all college constituencies. Input from everyone involved and affected, should be incorporated into any new proposals and plans. Feedback on outcomes should be disseminated throughout the college or university. Thirdly, change should be implemented incrementally, with the only constant being the need to change and reorganize when necessary, to reflect on what we do daily, why we do it, and how we do it. Change is not a singular event, but is rather a gradual process. It is important to listen and to engage as many people as possible in productive dialogue. However, in the end, it is the job of the enrollment and retention manager to implement reflective and constructive change as it relates to enrolling and retaining students.

Most organizational changes bring both covert and overt resistance. Some people, simply resist change no matter what. How should resistant staff members be handled? There are several available options. You can fire the person or persons. That gets everyone's attention in the short-term. However, this kind of action creates suspicion, fear, and resentment. Firing employees often creates a climate that is not conducive to producing positive results. People don't work effectively if they fear they will be fired. You could play to employees' strengths and reorganize their jobs to reflect those strengths. You can move resistant staff members within the organization, so that while not contributing to change, neither are they preventing it from occurring. Dissent is one thing. Sabotage is another and should not be tolerated.

There are other subtler, long-term solutions to the problem of dealing with resistant staff. Gradually fill vacant positions with current employees who are known to be more responsive to change or hire people who can be counted on to be open to new suggestions. Eventually, employees will get the message that resistance is not tolerated or rewarded and innovation and creativity are. This takes time and a great deal of patience on the part of the enrollment and retention manager. Set a realistic timetable for implementing the needed changes and get support from your superior. Keep your sense of humor. Don't personalize or take things too seriously. You cannot do it overnight. Remember Mark Twain's words, "People would rather die than change and most do." Remember you cannot produce change by yourself or in a vacuum. Change may take as long to institutionalize as it takes to develop a successful enrollment and retention management program. If we are lucky, this will be a never-ending process.

It is necessary to place the problems we face in higher education today in global, national, and societal perspective. Our problems are not isolated. Neither are the solutions. We all must be willing to adapt to the future, or we will not become a part of it. As Niccolo Machiavelli put it, "There is nothing more difficult to take in hand, more perilous to conduct, or more uncertain in its success than to take the lead in introducing a new order of things."

16

Conclusion

"My dear, we live in a time of transition," said Adam as he led Eve out of Paradise.

—W. Inge

What has been presented in this book are suggestions for enrolling students in colleges and universities and helping them, once enrolled, to reach their academic and career goals. As I cautioned in the opening pages of this publication, I do not believe that there is a great deal of magic in achieving a school's enrollment and retention objectives. While many enrollment and retention programs are based on research, I believe that computer simulations and sophisticated projection models and endless committee discussions will not bring students to our campuses and keep them there. A dedicated staff, led by effective and dynamic enrollment and retention management deans, who are working with relevant data, can and should produce the desired results.

Many colleges and universities are perhaps for the first time assessing who they are, what is central to their mission, what they value most, and how they will proceed to meet the challenges of our ever changing environment. The ultimate factors which will make the difference between those schools that will be successful in the future and those that will not is having a clear sense of mission, having the willingness to believe that risks must be taken if change is to occur, and believing that successful solutions to problems are possible.

Do not underestimate the need to embrace change as part of any successful enrollment and retention program. The willingness of faculty, staff and senior management to look not at what was but what will be in the future, the need to look at how we do business and see how we can do it in a different way, and the need to listen to our student-customers will provide the framework in which we conduct our activities. Underpinning all of this is the need to be responsive to our ever changing environment and world. However, the more change beckons, the more some things stay the same: students remain our customers and meeting their needs, our first priority.

Be good to yourselves. Refuse to accept the total responsibility for your school's enrollment and retention management problems. You may be, as an enrollment and retention manager, like an orchestra leader. However, you cannot be the entire orchestra. There are a great many players on your campus adding to, or subtracting from, the enrollment and retention of students. However, it is your responsibility to obtain the cooperation, and even enthusiasm, of as many people as possible in order to effectively administer programs that will result in more students coming to your school and more students staying until they have reached their educational objectives. Maintain good health and a good sense of humor. Develop a thick skin. Try not to personalize or be offended by angry faculty or staff who have their own agendas. Don't believe for one moment that you will always be able to please everyone. There will be many days when you won't be able to please even one person. Do your homework. Get the assistance of good people. Take risks. Fail. Learn from your failures. Try again. Learn from your successes. Celebrate them. And don't forget to laugh.

Two stonecutters were working on the reconstruction of St. Paul Cathedral in London when Sir Christopher Wren asked each what he was doing. The first replied, "I am cutting stone." The second answered, "I am building a cathedral." (From *Marketing Higher Education: A Practical Guide* by Robert Topor.)

POSTSCRIPT

The day after I finished writing this book, my job changed at Suffolk University. I was named vice president for development and enrollment, charged with combining the enrollment, retention, development, and alumni programs. For the past two years I have, in addition to learning the process of raising money and dealing with prospective donors and alumni, tried to incorporate and synergize the activities of the two divisions—enrollment, retention and development—so that they complement each other. While this is still a work in progress, my expanded role has given me an even greater appreciation for the work done "on the front end," in admissions and retention. I do, as was suggested in the book *Reinventing the University Managing and Financing of Higher Education*, view the process from student enrollment to alumni involvement as part of one, seamless, and transparent system. Satisfied students tend to become loyal alumni who are more likely to contribute to the life of a college or university after graduation and to contribute to its fund raising activities.

Over the past two years the divisions of enrollment, retention, and development, and alumni affairs have worked together and contributed to meeting the enrollment and fund raising goals of the university. This has been accomplished in a variety of ways and on many levels.

The staffs of the offices of undergraduate and graduate admission have identified during the time of recruitment and enrollment, families who may have an interest or ability to assist the university in a variety of ways. This information is given to the appropriate development and alumni affairs personnel at the time of enrollment. In prior years that information was made available only sporadically at the time of graduation. Time was lost in cultivating prospective donors.

The director of graduate admission works with both the director of alumni affairs and the director of corporations and foundations to help identify prominent alumni who could be instrumental in assisting with the enrollment, alumni, and fund raising activities of the university.

The director of financial aid works closely with the director of donor relations to steward scholarship programs and with the director of corporations and foundations to identify potential donors for additional scholarships.

The international student advisor strategizes with the director of international advancement to identify potential international donors to meet funding needs.

The director of alumni affairs works with the dean of enrollment management and the directors of undergraduate and graduate admission to identify graduates for the Alumni Ambassador Program which matches potential students with alumni. Each year, several hundred accepted students are contacted by alumni. International recruiters also meet with international alumni during their recruiting trips and conduct alumni activities with them.

The director of corporations and foundations attends retention management meetings and has been instrumental in securing grants for the university's retention activities.

Every five years the director of enrollment research conducts an alumni census. The information obtained from that survey is used by admission, alumni, and development personnel.

The office of creative services, which produces all of the publications for the university, works directly with the undergraduate and graduate admission offices, the alumni office, and the development office. The result has been a coordinated and "family" look for the brochures, publications, and magazines produced for the university.

The director of public affairs conducts monthly meetings with the staffs of the enrollment, retention, alumni affairs, and development offices to exchange information and determine how to use the information to meet the recruitment, retention, alumni, and fund raising activities of the university.

Although this type of arrangement and reporting structure is unique and would not be appropriate for many colleges and universities, it has proved effective and efficient at Suffolk University. There have been several benefits:

There is one person, a vice president for development and enrollment, to articulate the resource and financial needs of the university to alumni and potential donors.

Certain administrative functions have been combined. For example, there is one budget officer for both divisions. This has not only saved money but ended a duplication of certain activities.

The re-assignment of staff within the divisions can be easily facilitated. For example, the former international student advisor, previously employed in the enrollment and retention management division, was recently appointed the director of international advancement. She brings to this new position a wealth (no pun intended) of knowledge about potential international donors. She also identifies at the time of enrollment those families who have the potential to become major contributors and works with the director of donor research to match potential donors with funding needs.

Joint meetings allow staff to review current collaboration and propose synergy for future projects.

There are economies of scale when ordering paper, and supplies and when combining recruitment, alumni, and development trips.

This new administrative structure is like enrollment and retention management programs a work in progress. We will build on the synergy of the last two years to improve and further intergrate enrollment and retention management with fund raising and alumi activities.

Suffolk University is a small school with little bureaucracy which made this type of re-organization relatively easy to succeed. Although skeptical at first of the wisdom of combining these two divisions, I have come to appreciate and enjoy my expanded role and have come to the realization that the activities of enrollment and retention can only assist and enhance the activities of the alumni and development offices. This is an example of a new and different administrative paradigm which may very well mark the successful college or university of the future.

Appendix: Lists and Reports

The following lists and reports should be compiled each year by the Offices of Enrollment and Retention Management.

Total Student Enrollment

Undergraduate and Graduate Student Enrollment
Semester Comparative Enrollments
Semester Enrollment by School
Semester Full-time vs. Part-Time Enrollment
Semester to Semester Status Changes

Minority Student Enrollment

Minority Student Enrollment by School
Minority Student Enrollment by Status and Class
Minority Student Enrollment by Program and Gender
Comparison of New Minority Undergraduate and Graduate Student Enrollment
     and Recruitment Activities

International Student Enrollment

International Student Enrollment by School
International Student Enrollment by Status and Class

International Student Enrollment by Program and Gender
International Student Enrollment by Citizenship
Comparative Data on International Student Enrollment and Recruitment Activities

Continuing and Adult Students

Comparative Data of Enrollment of Adult Students by School, Program, Status, and Class, Day, or Evening Enrollment

Day and Evening Enrollment

Enrollment of Students in Day or Evening Classes
Evening Student Enrollment by Major, Credits, Program, and Class

Enrollment by Gender

Historical Enrollment by Gender
Undergraduate Student Enrollment by Class and Gender
Graduate Student Enrollment by Program and Gender

Out of State Enrollment

New Student Undergraduate and Graduate Enrollment from Out of State
Comparative Data on Out of State Enrollment and Recruitment Activities

Retention Statistics

Semester to Semester Retention by Major, Program, Ethnicity, Status, and Gender
Stopout Information Report
Leave of Absence Report
Student Withdrawal Report
Special Advisors Report
Academic Evaluation Reports
Mid-Term Verifications
Students Enrolled in Repeat Courses
Transcript Analysis Report
Academic Standing Lists
Students Subject to Dismissal Report
Students Subject to Probation Report
Analysis of Students with Excessive Incomplete or Withdrawal Grades
Lists of Students with Incomplete, Withdrawal, or Failing Grades for Financial Aid Compliance

Incomplete Grades Changed to Failing Grades
Departmental Retention Activity Reports

Graduation Statistics

Lists of Students Eligible to Apply for Graduation—Transcript Analysis and
    Verification
Annual Graduation Statistics by Program, Ethnicity, and Gender
Comparative Data on Graduation Statistics vs. Entering Scores and GPA
Lists of Students Graduating with Honors

Course Section Analysis

Course Section Analysis by Class Size
Course Section Demand by Time Slot
Space Utilization
Course Section Enrollments
Closed Course Sections Analysis
Cancelled Course Sections Analysis
Added Course Sections Analysis
Excess Demand for Sections
Faculty Course Load Report

Miscellaneous Reports

Academic Bulletin
Class Rosters
Lists for Honor Societies
Grade Distribution Lists
Immunization Lists
Registration Statements
Lists of Transcripts Issued
Final Grade Reports
Veterans Benefits Report

ANNUAL REPORT

It has been my experience over the years that while most schools require an
annual report at the end of the academic year from each of their administrative
offices, few senior administrators actually use the reports in the strategic planning process or to improve the activities of their divisions. Each year, usually
in January, we hold at Suffolk University a "review" session on the annual report. At this time, each program director reports on the progress of their objectives for the year as well as learn of any "holes" or difficulties in achieving those

goals. This process makes it possible to make any necessary adjustments in the mid-year point instead of waiting until the end of the academic cycle to initiait needed change and to assist the office staff in whatever way possible to achieve their goals for the year.

Each director is asked to report on the following:

Major accomplishments of the past year: Were the objectives of the previous year met? What were the results of the implementation of the previous year's goals?

Goals and objectives for the upcoming year: How can the office and programs be better managed? How can the office staff better serve the university's students, alumni, and donors?

The following are examples of the kind of information that should be reported by each director in the offices of enrollment and retention management.

Dean of Enrollment and Retention Management

The dean's report should analyze the effectiveness of the activities in recruitment, retention, corporate training, and new outreach and collaborative activities with other schools, both nationally and internationally. The following information should be presented.

- Percentage increase (decrease) in new student enrollment in all cohorts of students, undergraduate and graduate, by program
- Retention rates for all student cohorts, undergraduate and graduate, by program and comparison of retention rates to the previous semester and year
- Percentage increase (decrease) in total credit enrollment
- Gross revenue vs. net revenue analysis
- Analysis of new student cohorts, including corporate contracts, summer conferencing, international collaborations, and articulation agreements with other national, two-year institutions
- Analysis of all marketing plans by program and student cohort
- Analysis of financial aid packaging policies and the impact on enrollment and retention
- Review of publications for undergraduate and graduate programs, and corporate clients
- Analysis of the effectiveness of the advertising program on enrollment
- Personnel changes and reviews, and when appropriate, analysis of office and staff re-organization
- Identification of new markets for student enrollment
- Identification of student cohorts requiring additional or different retention outreach activities

Director of Undergraduate Admission

- Psychographic analysis of new student undergraduate enrollment, by market cohort and region and comparison of that data with marketing plans
- Analysis of the effects of financial aid policies on new student enrollment
- Analysis of the tracking process in student communication from the time of inquiry to enrollment
- Review of undergraduate admission publications
- Report on the outreach activities to local, national, and international guidance counselors
- Report on the outreach activities to local, national, and international two-year schools
- Review of the effectiveness of all undergraduate recruiting events, including fairs, forums, information sessions, open houses, and the like
- Review of all current and future articulation and two-plus-two agreements and how they can be strengthened in the future
- Review of faculty participation in the recruiting and admission processes
- Review of alumni participation in the recruiting and admission processes
- How to use technology in the admission process, that is applying for admission on-line

Director of Graduate Admission

- Psychographic analysis of graduate student enrollment by student cohort and program and comparison of that data with marketing plans
- Review of financial aid policies on graduate student enrollment
- Review of graduate school publications
- Review of the effectiveness of all graduate recruiting events, including local, national, and international fairs and forums and on-site and off-site special program seminars and information sessions
- Review of the effectiveness of graduate program advertising
- Analysis of outreach activities, including mentor matching and alumni involvement in the recruitment process
- Review and analysis of the effectiveness of the direct mail program
- The use of technology in the graduate admission process, that is, the use of e-mail, on-line application, and the like
- Results of graduate level collaborative agreements with local, national, and international institutions and organizations

Director of Financial Aid

- Review of financial aid procedures for undergraduate and graduate students and the impact of the policies on enrollment and retention
- Analysis of gross vs. net tuition revenues

- Review of student employment policies and procedures
- Review of the accuracy of all financial aid publications
- Review of entrance and exit counseling procedures
- Analysis of the Satisfactory Academic Progress procedures for all financial aid recipients
- Analysis of class attendance policies for refund regulations
- Review of financial aid award appeal process
- Review of interaction with development office personnel in selecting scholarship program recipients
- Review of compliance with all federal and state financial aid regulations
- Review of the use of technology in the financial aid process, that is, on-line application, and the like

Registrar

- Review of ways to improve student records management and archive student records
- Review of the policies and procedures for monitoring student attendance for compliance with federal regulations
- Review of student course audit procedures
- Process of providing enrollment reports on all student cohorts
- Review of retention reports on all student cohorts
- Review of course section analysis
- Graduation analysis
- Review of room scheduling lists including space utilization, and course section demand by time slot
- Analysis of data on course section enrollments, closed courses and cancelled courses
- Review of all course scheduling changes
- Analyze how to use technology in the registration process, including student registration, grade and transcript inquiry, and faculty access to class rosters on the World Wide Web, and explore the implementation of procedures for electronic transfer of class rosters, grade rosters, and graduation lists to faculty and staff

Director of Contract Training

- Compare the increase (decrease) in the number of training contracts with the previous year
- Analyze budget projections vs. actual revenue
- Analyze distance learning initiatives
- Prepare projections of future corporate clients—local, national, and international

Director of Enrollment Research and Planning

Analyze survey results, including:

- Undergraduate Student Satisfaction Survey, which analyzes students' needs and how the school responds to meeting those needs
- Admitted Student Questionnaire, which provides information on how prospective students view the school and how the college or university is rated by students in comparison to competitor schools
- Orientation/Marketing Survey should be administered to all new students who attended orientation programs. It should ask students to rate the university's admission, financial aid, and registration processes.
- Focus Group Analysis of undergraduate and graduate programs should ask small groups of students to provide feedback on the programs. This information should be given to the dean of enrollment and retention management and to each program director for information and follow-up.
- College Guides/Surveys for both national publications and internal reports should be completed by this office.
- Freshman Withdrawal Survey should ask accepted students who declined to enroll at the university which school they will be attending and how the university compares with their school of choice.
- Long Term Enrollment Projection Report should compare the future projections of enrollment with the gross and net revenue needs of the university.
- Budget Report should project student enrollment vs. actual enrollment and the relationship to the budget.
- Graduating Student Survey should ask graduating students to rate the services of the university. This information should be given to the president, vice presidents, deans, and program directors for information and follow-up.
- International Alumni Survey should ask international alumni to rate the university. This information should be shared with personnel in the alumni office and development.
- Stopout Survey should analyze which students were "lost" and why. This information should be shared with senior staff as well as members of the retention management committee.
- Resident Hall Survey should provide feedback to the residence hall staff on student satisfaction, dissatisfaction and recommendations to improve the facility.
- Analysis of the effects of the university's financial aid policies on enrollment and retention.
- Review of additional ways of using the World Wide Web to market the university.

Director of University Media and Creative Services

- Review of the activities of the staff of the office of university media and creative services and other offices throughout the university, including enrollment, retention, development, alumni affairs, and public affairs
- Review of the effectiveness of all university publications and advertising
- Analysis of the use of technology as it relates to media services throughout the college or university
- Maintaining and updating World Wide Web sites for all campus departments

Bibliography

Abraham, Jimmy. *Helping Students Ease into College*. Planning for Higher Education. 1992, 21 (1): 32–36.

Albright, John W. *Enrollment Management: Successor to Marketing or Its Antonym*. College and University, 1986. 61 (2): 114–117.

American College Personnel Association. *The Student Learning Experience*. American College Personnel Association, 1994.

Ashar, H., and R. Skenes. *Can Tinto's Student Departure Model Be Applied to Non-traditional Students?* Adult Education Quarterly. 1993, 43: 90–100.

Astin, Alexander. *Proposals for Change in College Administration*. San Francisco: Jossey-Bass, 1981.

———. *What Really Matters in College? Four Critical Years Revisited*. San Francisco: Jossey-Bass, 1993.

Baker, Robert W., and Kim L. Schultz. *Measuring Expectations About College Adjustment*. NACADA Journal. 1992, 12 (2): 23–32.

Balderston, Frederick E. *Managing Today's University*. San Francisco: Jossey-Bass, 1978.

Banta, Trudy W., and Associates. *Making a Difference: Outcomes of a Decade of Assessment in Higher Education*. San Francisco: Jossey-Bass, 1993.

Barker, Joel Arthur. *Future Edge*. New York: William Morrow and Company, Inc., 1992.

Barton, David. *Marketing Higher Education*. New Directions for Higher Education. San Francisco: Jossey-Bass, 1978.

Bean, John P. *Assessing and Reducing Attrition*. New Directions for Higher Education. March, 1986, 14 (1): 47–61.

Bloom, Allan. *The Closing of the American Mind*. New York: Scribner's Publishing Company, 1987.

Boger, Ruth E., and et al. *Involving Graduate Assistants in Student Retention Efforts.* College and University. Winter 1994: 100–103.

Bouse, G. A., and Don Hossler. *Studying College Choice: A Progress Report.* The Journal of College Admission. Winter, 1991: 11–6.

Boyer, Ernest L. *College: The Undergraduate Experience in America.* New York: Harper & Row, 1987.

Brooker, George, and Michael Noble. *The Marketing of Higher Education Problems and Solutions.* College and University. 1985, 60 (3): 191–200.

Bruker, Robert M., and Lawrence E. Taliana. *The Institutional Self-Study: First Step in a Viable Marketing Plan.* College and University. 1985, 61 (1): 32–42.

Bryant, S. *The Telephone: An Opportunity to Deepen Your Level of Customer Service.* Telemarketing. May, 1991: 68–69.

Bryce, Herrington, J. *Financial and Strategic Management for Nonprofit Organizations.* Englewood Cliffs, N. J. : Prentice Hall, 1992.

Budig, Gene A. *Higher Education Map for the 1990's.* Phoenix: Oryx Press, 1992.

Cabrera, Alberto F., and et al. *The Role of Finances in the Persistence Process: A Structual Model.* Research in Higher Education. 1992, 33 (5): 571–594.

Carnegie Council on Policy Studies in Higher Education. *Three Thousand Futures: The Next Twenty Years in Higher Education.* San Francisco: Jossey-Bass, 1980.

Cerney, Edward. *Marketing Techniques Employed by Private Liberal Arts Colleges.* College and University. 1992, 67 (3): 215–221.

Chait, Richard P. *Third and Long for Enrollment Managers: Life Inside the Pressure Cooker.* Change. September/October, 1987, 19 (5): 43–45.

Chan, Susan S. *Changing Roles of Institutional Research in Strategic Management.* Research in Higher Education. October, 1993, 34: 533–550.

Chance, William M. *Financial Aid's New Playing Field.* Academe. May/June, 1994, 80 (3): 21–25.

Cheit, Earl. *The New Depression in Higher Education.* New York: McGraw-Hill, 1971.

Clagett, C., and H. Kerr. *Tracking and Understanding Your Students.* Planning for Higher Education. Fall, 1993, 22: 9–15.

Collision, Michael N. K. *Private Colleges Unveil Tuition Discounts and Loans to Woo Middle-Income Students.* Chronicle of Higher Education. 1992, 38 (42): A27–A28.

Coomes, Michael D. *Understanding Students: A Developmental Approach to Financial Aid Services.* Journal of Student Financial Aid. 1992, 22 (2): 23–32.

Cronin, Joseph Marr, and Sylvia Quarles Simmons. *Student Loans Risks and Realities.* Westport, Conn. : Auburn House Publishing Company, 1987.

Dehne, George C. *Reinventing Student Recruitment.* Trusteeship. May/June, 1994, 2 (3): 11–15.

Devine, Joseph E. *Advising and Admission: Partners in Enrollment Management.* Journal of College Admissions. Fall, 1987, 117: 3–11.

Dolence, Michael G. *Strategic Enrollment Management and Planning.* Planning for Higher Education. 1988, 16 (3): 55–74.

———. *Evaluation Criteria for an Enrollment Management Program.* Planning for Higher Education. 1990, 18 (1): 1–14.

Drucker, Peter F. *The Effective Executive.* New York: Harper & Row, 1966.

Ehrenberg, R. G., and S. H. Murphy. *What Price Diversity? The Death of Need-Based Financial Aid at Selective Private Colleges and Universities.* Change. 1993, 25 (4): 64–73.

Eigne, Diane. *Student Retention: Many More Ideas.* College Student Journal. 1992, 26 (4): 472–475.

Ellen, D. *The Missing Quality Link: How to Implement Creative Innovation.* Tele-marketing. October, 1992: 59–62.

Esteban J. M., and C. J. Apel. *A Student's Eye View of Direct Mail Marketing.* The Journal of College Admission. Winter, 1992: 21–28.

Evans, Michael K. *Are You Ready for the Quarter-Million Dollar College Tuition?* Gentlemen's Quarterly. June, 1987: 119–123.

Flint, T. A. *Does Financial Aid Make Students Consider Colleges with a Wider Cost Range?* Journal of Student Financial Aid. 1991, 21 (2): 21–32.

Ford, Clinita. *Baker's Dozen for Retention Strategies.* AASCU Report. December, 1993: 9.

Ford, Jerry, and Shelia S. Ford. *Step-by-Step Guide to Producing a Comprehensive Academic Advising Handbook.* NACADA Journal. 1993, 13 (2): 50–51.

Frances, Carol. *Major Trends Shaping the Outlook for Higher Education.* American Association of Higher Education Bulletin. December, 1985: 3–7.

Frost, Susan H. *Developmental Advising Practices and Attitudes of Faculty Advisors.* NACADA Journal. 1993, 13 (2): 15–20.

Glennen, Robert E. *Expanding the Advising Team.* National Academic Advising Journal. Fall, 1989, 9 (2): 25–30.

Goldgehn, Lease. *Are U.S. Colleges and Universities Applying Marketing Techniques Properly and Within the Context of an Overall Marketing Plan?* Journal of Marketing for Higher Education. 1991, 3 (2): 39–61.

Grabowski, Stanley. *Marketing Higher Education.* Washington, D.C.: American Association for Higher Education, 1981.

Greenberg, Marvin W. *What's Happened to College Tuitions and Why: A View from a Public University.* College Board Review, Spring, 1988.

Grotrian, Harvey P. *New Strategies for Financing a College Education: What Are They and Will They Work?* Journal of Student Financial Aid. Spring, 1987: 45–48.

Grove, Josephine. *The Marketing Aspect of Enrollment Management: Evaluating the Impact on Recruitment and Retention in Institutions of Higher Education.* Master of Business Administration Thesis. Fontbonne College, 1992.

Gunn, Mary, and Richard Backes. *Avoidance of Pain: The Registrar's Role in Enrollment Management.* College and University. Spring, 1992, 67 (3): 183–186.

Hansen, Carl L. *Buying Students: Where Will It End?* College and University. 1986, 62 (1): 13–17.

Hardy, Cynthia. *Turnaround Strategies in Universities.* Planning for Higher Education. 1988, 16 (1): 9–23.

Henry, Thomas C., and Gregory R. Smith. *Planning Student Success and Persistence: Implementing a State Systems Strategy.* Community College Review. Fall, 1994, 22 (2): 26–36.

Himelstein, Howard C. *Early Identification of High-Risk Students: Using Noncognitive Indicators.* Journal of College Student Development. 1992, 33 (1): 89–90.

Hira, Tahira K. and Carla S. Brinkman. *Factors Influencing the Size of Student Debt.* Journal of Student Financial Aid. 1992, 22 (2): 33–50.

Hodgkinson, Harold. Paper on Demography and Higher Education. Prepared for the National Commission on Student Financial Assistance, Washington, D.C., 1982.

Hopkins, David, and William Massey. *Planning Models for Colleges and Universities.* Palo Alto, Cal.: Stanford University Press, 1981.

Hossler, Don. *Enrollment Management: An Integrated Approach.* New York: College Entrance Examination Board, 1984.

———. *Creating Effective Enrollment Management Systems.* New York: College Entrance Examination Board, 1986.

Hossler, Don, John P. Bean and associates. *The Strategic Management of College Enrollments.* San Francisco: Jossey-Bass, 1980.

Huneycutt, Archer W. *Marketing the University: A Role for Marketing Faculty.* College and University. Fall, 1990, 66 (1): 29–34.

Ihlanfeldt, William. *Achieving Optimal Enrollments and Tuition Revenues.* San Francisco: Jossey-Bass, 1981.

Jantzen, Jan. *Message.* Journal of Marketing for Higher Education. 1991, 3 (2): 129–138.

Johnson, Jody, and David Sallee. *Marketing Your College as an Intangible Product.* The Journal of College Admission. Summer, 1994, 144: 16–20.

Johnson, Sandra L., and Sean C. Rush. *Reinventing the University: Managing and Financing Institutions of Higher Education.* New York: John Wiley & Sons, Inc., 1995.

Jones, R. H. *Trends in Direct Mail Marketing.* The Journal of College Admission. Fall, 1991: 24–28, 133.

Kanter, R. M. *The Change Masters: Innovation for Productivity in the American Corporation.* New York: Simon & Schuster, 1983.

Kellaris, James J., and William K. Kellaris, Jr. *An Exploration of the Factors Influencing Students' Choice Decisions at Small Colleges.* College and University. 1988, 63 (2): 187–197.

Keller, George. *Academic Strategy: The Management Revolution in American Higher Education.* Baltimore: The Johns Hopkins University Press, 1983.

Kemerer, Frank R. *The Roles of Deans, Department Chairs, and Faculty in Enrollment Management.* New York: The College Board Review, Winter, 1984–1985, 134: 4–8.

Kiplinger, Austin. *America in the Global '90s.* Washington, D.C.: Kiplinger Books, 1990.

Kluepfel, Gail A., and others. *Involving Faculty in Retention.* Journal of Developmental Education. Spring, 1994, 17 (3): 16–27.

Kotler, Philip. *Marketing for Nonprofit Organizations.* Englewood Cliffs, N.J. : Prentice-Hall, 1982.

———. *Marketing Essentials.* Englewood Cliffs, N. J. : Prentice-Hall, 1984.

———. *Strategic Marketing for Education Institutions.* Englewood Cliffs, N. J. : Prentice-Hall, 1985.

Krotseng, Marsha V. *Designing Executive Information Systems for Enrollment Management.* New Directions for Institutional Research. Spring, 1993, 77: 49–61.

Lay, Robert, and John Maguire. *Identifying the Competition in Higher Education: Two Approaches.* College and University. 1980, 56 (1): 53–65

Leslie, Larry L. *What Drives Higher Education Management in the 1990s and Beyond? The New Era in Financial Support.* Journal for Higher Education Management. Winter/Spring, 1995, 10 (2): 5–16.

Levine, Arthur, and associates. *Shaping Higher Education's Future: Demographic Realities and Opportunities 1990-2000.* San Francisco: Jossey-Bass, 1989.

Levinson, Jay. *Guerilla Marketing.* Boston: Houghton Mifflin Company, 1984.

Litten, Larry H. *Avoiding and Stemming Abuses in Academic Marketing.* College and University. 1981, 56 (2): 105–122.

Lolli, Anthony, and James Scannell. *Admissions Market Research: An Alternative to Decline in the Eighties.* College and University. 1983, 58 (2): 135–151.

MacGowan, Sandra, ed. *Recruiting in the 1980s, Enrollment Management and Adult Students.* The Admission Strategist. 19 (11): 1–65.

Maguire, John, and Robert Lay. *Modeling the College Choice Process: Image and Decision.* College and University. 1981, 56 (2): 123–139.

Malone, Michael. *Formulating Academic Policy to Enhance Enrollment Management.* College and University. Spring, 1992: 166–168.

Mayhew, Louis B. *Surviving the Eighties: Strategies and Procedures for Solving Fiscal and Enrollment Problems.* San Francisco: Jossey-Bass, 1980.

McCorkle, Chester O., and Sandra Orr-Archibald. *Management and Leadership in Higher Education.* San Francisco: Jossey-Bass, 1982.

McPherson, M. S., and M. O. Shapiro. *Does Student Aid Affect College Enrollment? New Evidence on a Persistent Controversy.* The American Economic Review. March, 1991: 309–318.

Merante, Joseph A. *Organizing to Manage Enrollment.* College Board Review. Fall, 1987, 145: 14–17.

Miklich, Beverly A. *An Integrated Marketing Effort.* Journal of Marketing for Higher Education. 1988, 1 (1): 15–29.

Moll, Richard. *The Public Ivys.* New York: Viking Press, 1985.

Mortenson, Thomas G. *Family Income, Children, and Student Financial Aid.* American College Testing Program Student Financial Aid Report Series. April, 1989: 89–91.

Naisbitt, John. *Megatrends.* New York: Warner Books, 1982.

Newman, Frank. *Higher Education and the American Resurgence.* Princeton: Princeton University Press, 1985.

Noel, Lee. *Increasing Student Retention.* San Francisco: Jossey-Bass, 1987.

Ogilvy, David. *On Advertising.* New York: Crown Publishing, 1983.

Pace, Robert C. *Measuring Outcomes of College.* San Francisco: Jossey-Bass, 1979.

Pascarella, E., and P. Terenzini. *How College Affects Students: Findings and Insights from Twenty Years of Research.* San Francisco: Jossey-Bass, 1991.

Paulsen, Michael B. *Enrollment Management with Academic Portfolio Strategies: Preparing for Environment-Induced Changes in Student Preferences.* Journal of Marketing for Higher Education. 1990, 3 (1): 107–119.

Peters, Thomas. *The Pursuit of Wow!* New York: Random House, Inc., 1994.

Pollock, Charles R. *Student Retention Databases: An Important Element in Enrollment Management.* Paper presented at the Annual Meeting of the National Association of Student Personnel Administrators, 1989.

———. *The Status of Enrollment Management Programs within Four-Year Institutions of Higher Education.* College and University. Summer, 1989, 64 (4): 367–378.

Pride, William M. *Marketing Basic Concepts and Decisions.* Boston: Houghton Mifflin Company, 1983.

Rhoades, Gary. *Rethinking Restructuring in Universities.* Winter/Spring, 1995, 10 (2): 17–30.

Riehl, Richard J. *From Gatekeeper to Marketing Consultant: The Admission Officer's Changing Role.* College and University. 1982, 57 (3): 327–329.

Ries, Al. *Positioning: The Battle for Your Mind.* New York: McGraw-Hill, 1981.

Riesman, David. *On Higher Education: The Academic Enterprise in an Era of Rising Consumerism.* San Francisco: Jossey-Bass, 1980.

Robinson, L. F. *Showcasing the Campus Visit to Improve Student Recruitment.* The Journal of College Admission. Summer, 1991, 132: 30–31.

Rourke, Francis, and Glenn Brooks. *The Managerial Revolution in Higher Education.* Baltimore: The Johns Hopkins University Press, 1966.

Ryland, Elizabeth B., and et al. *Selected Characteristics of High-Risk Students and Their Enrollment Persistence.* Journal of College Student Development. January, 1994, 35: 54–58.

Sevier, Robert A. *Writing a Marketing Plan.* College and University. Summer, 1989.

———. *Image Is Everything Strategies for Measuring, Changing and Maintaining Your Institution's Image.* College and University. Winter, 1994: 60–75.

134   Bibliography

———. *Marketing College Publications for Today's Students.* The Journal of College Admission. Winter, 1990, 126: 23–28.
Seymour, Daniel. *Once Upon a Campus: 14 Lessons for Improving Quality.* Phoenix: Oryx Press, 1995.
Slaughter, Shelia. *Criteria for Restructuring Postsecondary Education.* Journal for Higher Education Management. Winter/Spring, 1995, 10 (2): 31–44.
Smith, S. *How Do Students Choose a Particular College? A Survey of Admitted Students: 1990.* College Journal. 1991, 25: 482–488.
Smith, Virginia Carter, and Susan Hunt. *The New Guide to Student Recruitment Marketing.* Washington, D.C.: Council for the Advancement and Support of Education, 1986.
St. John, Edward P. *Workable Models for Institutional Research on the Impact of Student Financial Aid.* Journal of Student Financial Aid. 1992, 22 (3): 13–26.
———. *The Impact of Student Financial Aid: A Review of Recent Research.* Journal of Student Financial Aid. 1991, 21 (1): 18–31.
Starr, S. Frederick. *A President's Message to Planners.* Planning for Higher Education. Fall, 1993, 22: 16–22.
Terenzine, P. T., and E. T. Pasacrella. *Living with Myths: Undergraduate Education in America.* Change. 1994, 26 (1): 28–32.
———. *The Transition to College: Diverse Students, Diverse Stories.* Research in Higher Education. February, 1994, 35: 57–74.
TERI. *Taxing Matters College Aid, Tax Policy & Educational Opportunity.* Boston: The Education Resource Institute, 1997.
———. *College Debt and the American Family.* Boston: The Education Resource Insitute,1995.
Tinto, Vincent. *Leaving College: Rethinking the Causes and Cures of Student Attrition.* Chicago: University of Chicago Press, 1987.
Topor, Robert. *Marketing Higher Education: A Practical Guide.* Washington, D.C.: Council for Advancement and Support of Education, 1983.
———. *Institutional Image: How to Define, Improve, Market It.* Washington, D.C.: Council for Advancement and Support of Education, 1986.
Townsley, Michael K. *A Strategic Model for Enrollment-Driven Private Colleges.* Journal for Higher Education Management. Winter/Spring, 1993, 8 (2): 57–66.
Trawick, Frederick I., and Thomas L. Powers. *Improving Customer Service in the Admission Process: A Survey at Public and Private Institutions.* The Journal of College Admission. Fall, 1992, 137: 13–17.
Treadwell, D. R., and J. E. Keller. *How Much Really Do Words and Images Matter in the Student Recruitment Process?* The Journal of College Admission. Winter, 1991: 23–26.
Urban, Davis J. *Qualitative Research Applications in Developing Marketing Plans.* Journal of Marketing for Higher Education. 1990, 3 (1): 29–47.
Walker, Donald E. *The Effective Administrator.* San Francisco: Jossey-Bass, 1979.
Wilder, Joyce S. *Attrition in Higher Education: A Tragic Waste of Human Resources.* College Student Journal. 1992, 26 (3): 340–344.
Williams, William G. *Enrollment Strategy.* Charlottesville, VA. : Shore Publishing Company, 1980.
Wonders, Thomas J., and James F. Gyure. *Opportunistic Markets in Higher Education.* Journal of Marketing for Higher Education. 1991, 3 (2): 1–16.

Index

About the Author

MARGUERITE J. DENNIS is Vice President for Development and Enrollment at Suffolk University in Boston.

ISBN 0-89789-591-6

90000>

9 780897 895910

EAN

HARDCOVER BAR CODE